EIGHT GREAT IDEAS

Simple Ways to
Transform Your Teaching

Rick Morris
Creator of New Management

Other Books by Rick Morris

New Management Handbook: A Step-by-Step Guide for Creating a Happier, More Productive Classroom
Tools & Toys: Fifty Fun Ways to Love Your Class
Class Cards: How to Put Your Class in the Palm of Your Hand

Eight Great Ideas: Simple Ways to Transform Your Teaching
Copyright © 2007 by Rick Morris
Revised Second Edition 2011
Revised Third Edition 2013

New Management
4079 Governor Drive #330
San Diego, California 92122

For information, you can call us at:
(858) 455-6000

or send e-mail to:
rick@newmanagement.com

or visit our website at:
www.newmanagement.com

I.S.B.N. 1-889236-10-1

Cover design
Len Torres

Back cover caricature
Nate Robb

Editor
Laura Decorte

Not that we are sufficient of ourselves to think of anything
as being from ourselves, but our sufficiency comes from God.
—II Corinthians 3:5

*For all of the teachers who
have expressed their support
over the many years that
I've been on the road
sharing my ideas...*

this book is for you.

Table of Contents

Acknowledgements

The last book I wrote, the *New Management Handbook: Creating a Happier, More Productive Classroom*, was dedicated to my sweet wife, Debbie. Love you, babe.

The book before that one, *Tools & Toys: Fifty Fun Ways to Love Your Class*, was for my son, Ben. What a fine young man he is.

And the first book I wrote, *Class Cards: How to Put Your Students in the Palm of Your Hand*, was for Gladys Berner, the teacher who gave me the original idea. Gladys was a mentor in the truest sense of the word.

This one, though, is for all of the teachers who—either speaking with me at the end of a seminar or sending me an e-mail days, weeks, or months later—have expressed their heart-felt appreciation for the ideas I've created that help to make the classroom a better place for teachers and students. I don't think it's even possible to express my gratitude. Please know that I am blessed by your words and grateful for your continued support.

I'd like to add a special thanks to one teacher in particular, Bonnie Harris of Lake Gregory Elementary School. Bonnie and I conferred through email about each of the eight chapters in this book. It was a great comfort to listen to another teacher's insight, perspective, and encouragement during what was sometimes a lonely endeavor. And the suggestions she offered about how the ideas were being presented, which I incorporated, have helped to make this a better book.

In the last book I offered my thanks to God for the gifts He's given me for problem solving and organization; but, how can I not give my thanks once again?

You're right. I can't.

Thanks, Lord.

*I wake up every morning
determined both to change the world
and have one heck of a good time.
Sometimes this makes planning the day
a little difficult.*

—*E. B. White*

About This Book

Eight Great Ideas is a funny book.

Not ha-ha funny, but funny because it's an odd collection of eight separate ideas explained in eight separate chapters.

Two of the eight chapters—*Sentence Strips* and *Homework Made Easier*—were already in print as 16-page teaching guides. Having written one of them in 1992 and the other one in 1997, they were both in serious need of updating. So I subjected each to a rewrite, included them in this book, and will now retire the original editions. May they rest in peace.

The other six chapters are ideas that, although significant in their own right, would not warrant a book of their own. But as opposed to letting the ideas reside in some nether world of sometimes-shared-at-seminars-but-not-available-in-print, I decided to build a book around them.

Now then, it has never been my desire to upset the hall monitors of educational conformity; nonetheless, some of the ideas in this book are not based upon traditional pedagogy. They are, instead, based upon my own quest for a better way. In order to be the best teacher I could be, I was willing to go in a new direction, to try a new strategy, to break new ground. It was nothing more than a reflection of that whole John Cotton Dana thing in which he stated, "Anyone who dares to teach must never cease to learn."

Or, as Confucius put it:

> *Only through education does one come to be dissatisfied with his own*
> *knowledge, and only through teaching others does one come to real-*
> *ize the uncomfortable inadequacy of his knowledge. Being dissatisfied*
> *with his own knowledge, one then realizes that the trouble lies with*
> *himself, and realizing the uncomfortable inadequacy of his knowledge*
> *one then feels stimulated to improve himself. Therefore, it is said,*
> *"The processes of teaching and learning stimulate one another."*

It's my hope that you will find the eight ideas in this book to be not only stimulating but also worthy of being used in your own classroom.

—Rick Morris
  San Diego, California
  June 25, 2013

Five Basic Student Needs

power
love
fun
freedom
safety

The margin icon to the left relates to the five basic student needs William Glasser identified in his book *The Quality School Teacher*. It's Glasser's belief that these needs must be met in the classroom in order for students to become truly active participants. The reason this is critical, he states, is that an increase in student involvement will lead, in time, to a corresponding increase in student achievement.

power
love
fun
freedom
safety

As you'll soon discover, the strategies contained in this book were designed to help you bring Glasser's philosophy to life in your own classroom. In an effort to highlight this fact, I've placed student need icons in the margin next to the passages that allude to one of them and have highlighted the specific need being met. Most of the references are rather obvious; nonetheless, some of them are a bit more subtle. The icons are there to help you uncover the subtle, more obscure references. (That's love, baby.)

power
love
fun
freedom
safety

By the way, you'll sometimes find a passage that actually refers to two or more of the needs. When that does occur, the margin notation will indicate it.

Old School

If you've attended a New Management seminar in the past, you will most likely recall comments I made about Old School practices. For those of you who haven't attended one—or attended one and are drawing a blank—here's a quick explanation.

Old School refers to teaching practices that have been used for years on end with little regard to their actual effectiveness. They are the strategies and dialogues your own teachers may have used when you were a student. Although some Old School concepts are good—holding students accountable, to name just one—a lot of them need to be retired.

Realistically speaking, though, the only way they'll be put to pasture is if someone comes up with a better way to go. I think I may have found a few ways.

Independence vs Obedience

One of those better ways to go has to do with building a classroom culture that is based on independence. Helping students develop initiative along with self-direction goes a long way to creating a happy, productive classroom.

You'll find a number of ideas and strategies in this book that will help you to promote and encourage independence.[†] Just be prepared for the fact that students, for the most part, are not used to being in charge of themselves and will need some time in order to develop the requisite self-control. (The next section on Conditioning addresses this.)

---

†   Chapter 4, for instance, used to be called *How to Use Music for Management*. Its new title is *Using Music for Student Independence*.

Conditioning

One thing I've learned during my years of classroom teaching and seminar presenting is that students, and their teachers, have become conditioned to how school operates. Some of this conditioning is good; some of it is not so good. But, good or bad, the important factor is that conditioning is a powerful force.

Poor behavior or a bad attitude is the result of years of conditioning and cannot be undone overnight. It's going to take a deft hand, a patient touch, and the understanding that teaching, for the most part, is a crock-pot affair; real growth and development require time. Unfortunately, we live in a microwave society in which everyone is obsessed with the quick fix. The team is losing? Fire the coach. The dog is barking? Kick him.

Truth be told, when it comes to replacing bad conditioning with better conditioning, it's going to take more than just a kick.

Whether we're talking about sentence structure or appropriate behavior while on a field trip, learning—and the teaching that is supposed to precede it—sometimes takes longer than we think it should. This is why I encourage teachers, especially new ones, to keep their eyes on the horizon; to anticipate a future in which your students are more successful and productive. After all, education is not an event. It's a process.

This long-term approach is something I've maintained for most of my career. In fact, whenever I began a new school year, I was never too worried about the first day. My years of teaching had shown me that we were going to get through our first day together just fine. But do you know what I was already thinking about on that first day of the new year? I was thinking about where my students were going to be in one week after I'd had a chance to introduce some simple procedures and had begun the important process of reconditioning. I was thinking about where we were going to be in one month after the procedures had been learned and the reconditioning had begun to have an effect. I was thinking that I had them all year and would need to remain calm and exercise patience.

> *I was thinking that a tree will not produce fruit*
> *until its roots have had a chance to grow.*

There will be times when it seems as if the progress you are making with some of your students is so small that it's not worth the effort. You begin to get frustrated and feel like throwing in the towel. It's the Old School, "I've had it with you!" syndrome.

When you feel this way, don't give up and don't give in. Overcoming bad conditioning takes time, but it will be time well spent. If it helps, think of this time and effort as an investment that, over time, will yield dividends.

power
love
fun
freedom
safety

Reality: Students, for the most part, want to do well. They just need someone—a loving, consistent, dependable someone—to walk beside; someone who will help them stay on the straight-and-narrow until they have developed the ability to walk that path alone.

Conversations & Thoughts

As was done in the *New Management Handbook*, dialogues are used throughout this book to: 1) help clarify procedures; and 2) provide some modeling of how I interact with students. There are times, however, when I'm not showing what a person is saying but, instead, what that person is thinking. To indicate that the words are a thought, they will be embraced by two brackets.

[Hmmmm. I hope I made myself clear about showing thoughts.]

Back Cover Table of Contents

One last thing.

On the back cover of this book, you'll find a second Table of Contents. It's nothing more than a list of the titles of each chapter.

power
love
fun
freedom
safety

I just thought you might appreciate having a quick and easy way to find a specific chapter instead of having to flip through a bunch of pages in the front of the book because you're trying to find the actual Table of Contents which, by the way, is located on page *v*.

FYI: Page *v* is page 5 for those of us who took a language other than Latin in high school.

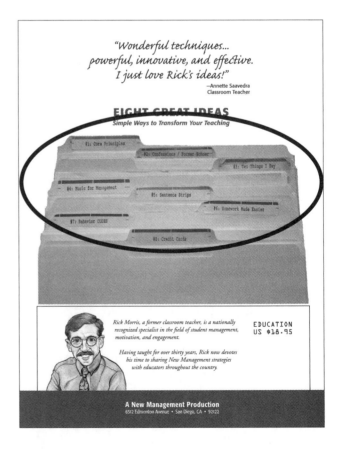

Chapter One

Core Principles

Confessions of a Former Echoer

The Top Ten Things I Said

Using Music for
Student Independence

Sentence Strips
Cut-and-Paste Paragraphs

Homework Made Easier

Behavior CODES

Credit Cards

Only a teacher?
Thank God I have a calling
to the greatest profession of all!
I must be vigilant every day lest I lose
one fragile opportunity to improve tomorrow.

—Ivan Welton Fitzwater

Chapter 1
Core Principles

◆ ◆

Goals for this chapter:

☑ Learn about the six Core Principles for being an effective teacher.

☑ Discover simple ways you can apply these principles in your own classroom.

☑ Develop your own Core Principles to add to the ones I've shared.

◆ ◆

As I worked on this book back in 2006 during a leave of absence, I spent a lot of time reflecting on my thirty-one years of teaching. And the more I thought about those years, the more I came to realize that there were a handful of beliefs which had proven to be critical to my success and to the ultimate success of my students. I now refer to these beliefs as Core Principles and have identified six of them.[†]

 You have safe relationships with your students.

 Your words equal your actions.

 You are fair, firm, and consistent.

 You can focus your attention.

 Your classroom is manageable for everyone.

 Your students are problem solvers.

Although time and pages do not allow for an in-depth analysis of each one, I would like to offer a glimpse into the thinking that produced these principles. So, let's turn the page and take a closer look.

---

† There might be another six. Who knows?

Core Principle 1
You have safe relationships with your students.

For years, educators have talked about the "teachable moment." However, I've come to realization that the "relationship moment" is of greater significance. In fact, the hard numbers that were generated in a study by Peart & Campbell (1999) make the point.

FACTORS THAT CONTRIBUTE TO STUDENT ACHIEVEMENT

— *quality of human interaction (relationships) in the school (78%)*

— *issues over which the school has no control (6%)*

— *teaching techniques and lessons presented (16%)*

power
love
fun
freedom
safety

Although we've known for years that students do better academically for teachers they like, seeing the relationship factor receive such a big slice of the pie is food for thought. That's not to say we can sit around singing *Kumbaya* and everyone will become magically proficient. After all, mastery of subject matter requires direct instruction, student engagement, application of knowledge, and follow-up tutoring.

The relationship, though, is what I call an achievement multiplier. It can transform a classroom into a vibrant, dynamic, warm, and accepting place in which true growth and development is able to flourish. Please don't take this the wrong way, but I think it has more to do with knowing your students than knowing the subject matter.

For instance, when you first see a student, what is your initial response?

Did you do the homework last night?

Good to see you. How are you doin' today?

power
love
fun
freedom
safety

Without wanting to belabor the obvious, all I'm saying is that you should treat your students the way you would want a teacher to treat your own children. Speaking of which...

Safety is a Need
A key component to building a relationship with any student is making yourself safe to be around. Although this is relatively easy to do when things are going well, the true test is how you act when things aren't going so well. A partial indication of your character, as a teacher, can be measured by your grace under pressure.

power
love
fun
freedom
safety

One surefire way to maintain your cool and keep yourself safe is to visualize the parents of your students in the room with you. The mental image of Mom and Dad standing behind the student you are addressing about misbehavior should really help to keep you from saying anything inappropriate. Because sometimes, it's not about building relationships. It's about protecting and maintaining the ones you've already developed.

Looking for the Good

power
love
fun
freedom
safety

Love, as we already know, is a student need. And in the classroom, love is nothing more than looking for the good in a student. If you can do that—find the good others may have missed—you'll be on your way to building relationships. So, whenever you can, give 'em some love, give 'em some respect, and show some appreciation for who they are.

The Bigger Picture

While you're at it, see if you can avoid using the microscope that only focuses on the academic ability of the student and look, instead, through the lens which enables you to see the whole child.

This "whole child" approach is especially important for the underachievers in your room who are usually the most difficult students with whom to bond. Over the years, they've had less-than-satisfactory experiences when it comes to classwork and lessons. This lack of success keeps feeding and reinforcing their negative perceptions of teachers in general and school in particular which, in turn, makes it less likely they'll connect well with their new teacher.

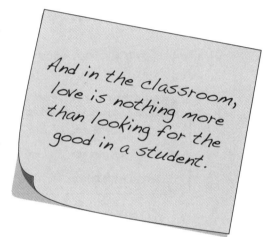

And in the classroom, love is nothing more than looking for the good in a student.

The sadly predictable outcome is that the underachiever is never able to develop a strong relationship with the teacher which further impacts the acquisition of new skills and causes him to fall farther behind. Small wonder some of them just give up and drop out.

So what do you do with these students? How do you reach out and connect with them?

power
love
fun
freedom
safety

You build a working relationship with them. Have them take care of some job that needs to be done in the classroom. Ask them to help you with a tedious task. ("I'll put the pages together and you staple them. Okay?") It could be a big thing or a small one. It doesn't matter.

By inviting your students to take care of non-academic tasks and then expressing your sincere appreciation for their efforts, you will be laying the foundation for a long-term relationship.[†]

And even though the relationship was initially developed through classroom management situations, it will eventually have a positive impact upon the academic relationship that will be so crucial to the child's overall success and achievement.

---

†   That's assuming, of course, that the child did a good job. If that wasn't the case, a private conversation regarding how the job should be done would be in order. This kind of "relationship moment" will contribute to the reconditioning campaign he's going to experience this year as you help him learn to be successful in all facets of classroom life.

Core Principle 2

Your words equal your actions.

When your words equal your actions, students will learn to trust what you say. Sounds simple, doesn't it? Actually, it *is* simple as long as you bear in mind that students are not used to teachers meaning what they say. They've been around adults who do a lot of talking but not much more. Couple this with Piaget's findings that children learn through what they experience, and you end up with a recipe for frustration.

> FRUSTRATED TEACHER
> *Class, you need to stop talking or I'm going to have to ask you to stop talking again.*

A little over the top, I know, but it speaks to the point I'm trying to make. If you'd prefer a more realistic example, here you go.

BAD CONDITIONING

What they heard: *You have 15 minutes to complete this assignment.*

What they experienced: *The teacher got distracted helping students; 15 minutes became 20 minutes.*

What they learned: *Why work hard? We'll have more time than the teacher said we would.*

Yes, that was more realistic but you shouldn't think it was any better. It was just as bad as the one about talking. Care for another example?

MORE BAD CONDITIONING

What he heard: *I'm going to call your parents, young man, and tell them about your misbehavior in class.*

What he experienced: *The teacher felt that the threat to call was enough; the call to the parents was not placed.*

What he learned: *I can ignore my teacher. Her bark is far worse than her bite.*

No more, Rick. Please. Just cut to the chase and give me your best advice about how I can make sure my words equal my actions.

Okay, then.

Here it is:

MacKenzie's book will literally change the way you interact with your students. Among other things, you'll learn that the two basic discipline styles used by most teachers—punitive or permissive—don't work. Never have, never will.

The punitive teacher employs words that are mean while the permissive teacher employs words that border on pleading. What's missing from both is the action that children need in order to learn.

One of the great things about MacKenzie's book is how real it is. You'll read dozens of observations he made of teachers interacting with students regarding common misbehavior. You'll see why the punitive teacher goes wrong and why the permissive teacher can't get the job done. You'll also see why the "action teacher" has the greatest success.

So, trust me on this one. Buy the book. Read the book. You'll be happy you did because it will show you how to ensure that your words equal your actions.

When...then...

The only issue I have with the book is that the "action teacher" in an observation will sometimes use the word "if" when talking with students. The one example that stands out occurs at recess when a teacher is talking to students who are playing a karate game that had already been banned from the playground.

> MRS. TAYLOR
> An action teacher:
>> *Guys, you'll have to choose another game to play. That game is not allowed. If you play it again, you'll have to sit out the rest of recess on the bench.*

In that situation, I would have used "when" in place of "if" and "then" to introduce the consequence. "If" is such a weasel word. There's too much room for kids to deny the reality of the interaction. As soon as you say "if," they start to run through the possibilities.

> *[If you catch me.]*
> *[If you see me.]*
> *[If you really do back up your words and make me sit on the bench.]*

It's a minor point, I'll grant, but an important one just the same. "When...then..." is clearer and implies a direct relationship between words, deeds, and actions.

> MR. MORRIS
> Ever the action teacher:
>> *Gentlemen, that game is not allowed. And when you play that game, then you'll end up sitting on the bench. Please find something else to do. Thanks, boys.*

And if they were to play the game again after I had advised them of their rights and responsibilities? I would have walked them over to the bench and had them sit down. The action—sitting on the bench—would have started them on a Journey of Understanding in which they learned that Mr. Morris meant what he said. He was an action guy, and it was best to heed his words. This awareness would have a profound impact upon their future behavior. And, as educators, we're always thinking about the future.

Important: MacKenzie states that students gather research on their teachers. That's kind of a scary thought, don't you think? A statement such as that has got to make you pause and ponder the information your own students are gathering about you.

Core Principle 3

You are fair, firm, and consistent.

Here's what I've learned about being fair, firm, and consistent in the classroom: it's really hard to achieve on your own; especially the consistency piece. This is primarily due to the fact that: 1) we are creatures of emotion, and 2) we work in very complex social environments. Maintaining a sense of balance and equilibrium is going to require something more than willpower or feng shui.

What You Need

In order to be successful, every teacher needs a system of classroom management. I can state this with authority because, for my first five years of teaching, I didn't have one. There were no procedures for getting the attention of my students, for collecting assignments, or for calling upon students in an equitable fashion. It was just me trying to wing it, and the results were not pretty.

Student numbers became the solid foundation on which I was able to stand and deliver in a fair, firm, and consistent manner.

Then, in year six, I started to use student numbers.[†] Eureka! I was suddenly empowered to be the consistent teacher I knew my students needed. Over time, I was able to create a variety of student number tools that not only helped me develop an awareness of how each of my students was doing, but also use that awareness to inspire them onward.

Student numbers became the solid foundation on which I was able to stand and deliver in a fair, firm, and consistent manner. It allowed me to teach using my natural style—Mr. Rogers with a sense of humor—without being taken advantage of by my students. The message my new system sent to them was clear and unmistakable: Mr. Morris knew what was goin' on.

power
love
fun
freedom
safety

The guesswork was gone; the drama had fled. In its place was a happy, productive room in which the teacher and the students worked together to be the best they could be.

Teacher Leadership

The other thing you need is a bit more difficult to achieve, but it can be done. What you need is to be a good role model for your students. Before you roll your eyes—if you haven't already—allow me to admit that I know it sounds cliché. Nonetheless, someone has to be able to rise above the norm and act in ways that are both noble and dignified. Someone has got to lead the way to a better place. That someone needs to be you.

---

†   If you haven't tried student numbers, you're in for a treat. I can almost guarantee it will revolutionize your classroom and provide you with a level of control you would not have thought possible. Check out the *New Management Handbook* for step-by-step directions on how to transform your classroom into a better place.

Being Firm

This is not too tough if you've followed the advice on the previous page about being consistent. (And don't forget the suggestion on page 6 about reading MacKenzie's book.)

Just remember two simple things:

"No" means no. ("I've got a whole bag full of 'no' for you, so stop asking.")
Being firm does not mean being rude or disrespectful.

A Word About the Word "Fair"

Fair is a word that students have learned to use against their teachers when they don't get what they want.

STUDENT
Full of bluster and petulance:
That's not fair! She always gets to _____.

Fill in the blank with any of a hundred different things. This is why I take the time to define the word "fair" for my students. (Fair is not always equal; fair is what's right.)

MR. MORRIS
Speaking privately with the plaintiff:
Actually, it was fair. I needed someone who had already finished the vocabulary assignment. She had. You still needed to finish yours. And did you miss the fact that I used the Class Cards to select a helper? The Cards are as fair as I can get.
Pause for it to sink in.
Maybe next time, eh?

By using my set of Class Cards,† I was able to avoid any unintentional bias that may have occurred if I had chosen a helper on my own. The Cards effectively eliminate the need for me to play—and most likely lose—the Old School game called, "I need a helper."

power
love
fun
freedom
safety

Reality check: Accept the fact that you are not going to be able to please all of them at the same time. But, if you work at it, you'll be able to find your way through the mine field of disgruntled students and create a safe place in which everyone can feel included and appreciated.

You Know You're a Fair Teacher If...

You don't jump to conclusions.
You assume the best about your students.
You listen to both sides of an argument.
You always try to do what's right.
You forgive them as readily as you forgive yourself.

---

† *Class Cards* is the name of the first book I wrote back in 1988. It describes in detail how to use 3x5 index cards with a student's name written on each card. My set of cards is one of the five things I would never teach without.

Core Principle 4

You can focus your attention.

This is one of the easier principles to develop. Not only that, but your ability to focus will get better the more you work at it. But before I get too far ahead of myself, I should probably stop and explain what I mean by the statement, "You can focus your attention."

In its simplest form, it translates thusly:

Don't speak to everyone about the actions of a few.

A variation on that theme would be:

Shelter and protect the compliant students.

Let me share a strategy that epitomizes this principle. It's called the Freedom List.

power
love
fun
freedom
safety

My students had the option of working just about anywhere they wished in the class-room.† They could move to study, complete an assignment, or read independently.

Being a realist, I was experienced enough to know that some of my students would take advantage of this freedom and use it as an opportunity to goof off. So I posted a list of names in the room and labled the list: *Work Away.* Whenever a "mover" got off task—and I was all about on-task behavior—I called them over to the list.

> MR. MORRIS
> Calmly drawing a line through the student's name on the list:
> *That wasn't very productive. Please return to your seat.*

By drawing a line through just one name, I was focusing my attention. And by revoking the moving privilege—a line through your name meant you couldn't move until a new list was posted on Monday—I was able to fulfill Core Principle #2: Your words equal your actions. Sweet.

power
love
fun
freedom
safety

By the end of that first week, there might have been less than a dozen names not scratched out. Okay by me. And it was definitely okay with the students who were still allowed to work where they wished. *The bottom line:* My focus was their gain.

An Old School teacher, having issued multiple warnings to a dozen students over the course of a day or two, would eventually reach the breaking point and snap.

> OLD SCHOOLER
> *NO MORE MOVING AROUND! YOU'RE JUST GOOFING OFF!*

---

† The only requirement was that the move did not hinder a student from being productive. Not productive? Back to your seat, please.

The raised voice and the angry words are bad enough. The truly troubling aspect, though, is the handful of students feeling disrespected.

> RESPONSIBLE STUDENT
>> *[What??? I wasn't goofing off. I always work hard. And I like leaning*
>> *against the wall to read. Man, I hate it when teachers act this way.]*

By using the Freedom List, I was able to restrict the access of the students who had gotten off-task outside, yet allow the self-disciplined to retain their privilege.

On Monday—since I was a fresh-start kind of guy—I'd post a list. Everyone was back in the game. However, if you moved but didn't stay on-task, you were going to be called over and asked to draw a line through your name. It was up to you.

Protecting Relationships

The other huge advantage to focusing is that it will really help you to maintain good relationships with your more responsible students. Although this is normally easier to do than it is with the knuckleheads, it's important that you make an effort to do so. You would never want the students who *are* exercising self-discipline to pay for the sins of the students who aren't. (Remember Core Principle #3? You are <u>fair</u>, firm, and consistent.)

Variation on a Theme

By the way, if the example just given does not match your learning environment, don't toss it aside. Come up with a substitute. For example, maybe you have a special place in your room where students can sit and read. If that's the case, post a list near this area and revoke the privilege of anyone who does not follow your agreed upon standards.

> YOU
>> Acting upon your previously stated words as you address two students:
>>> *This area is for reading only. When you talk, then you have to leave. Draw a line*
>>> *through your names, please.*

Jot Down a Name

Whenever you are in the middle of something and a student is acting inappropriately, jot down the student's name. Just the mere act of writing, without a word being spoken, will have an impact. Then, later on when you are free to meet privately, call the student aside.

> YOU
>> Speaking calmly yet firmly:
>>> *When you do not pay attention on the carpet, then I will need to see you at recess time.*

It won't take too many of these interactions before your students begin to realize they can't hide from your all-seeing, yet discerning, eye.

Core Principle 5

Your classroom is manageable for everyone.

A buddy of mine who was a shop teacher—back in the day when they taught kids how to work with wood and metal—said to me one day, "Putting oil on rust is like putting water on a fire." In the regular classroom, the oil is the procedure and the rust is one of those tedious, troublesome things that can wear us out and grind us down.

Let me give you a silly example from my own classroom that illustrates this concept.

My set of classroom keys was composed of two padlock keys and two door keys. The padlock keys, to open the gates, were easy. Both of the keys, and the padlocks they unlocked, were different. When I came upon a padlock, I always knew which key to grab.

The door keys, on the other hand, weren't as easy. Other than a slight difference in how the teeth were cut, they were identical. One was for my classroom, and the other was for the men's restroom. Because of their similarities, I found myself fumbling back and forth between the two keys whenever I attempted to unlock my classroom door. Go through that 12 times a day and you can turn a minor nuisance into a major annoyance.

Fig. 1-1
The fact that I can identify my classroom key at a glance reduces my stress on a daily basis.

So I bought a key ring. Not the kind you put keys on but the little molded rubber thing that goes around the big end of a key. By putting one on the key for my classroom door, I eliminated the fumbling. Forever.

Now, I warned you it was silly; but, I think it's indicative of how I operated in the classroom. The annoyance caused by having two nearly identical keys was solved by removing the source of the frustration. And that, at its most fundamental level, is the secret to my problem-solving success.

*Deconstruct a problem until you get to
the core issue and then resolve that issue.*

By making the key for my classroom door visibly different from his twin brother, the restroom key, I was able to easily identify the correct key whenever I needed to. And the fact that I was no longer subjecting myself to that little inconvenience kept me fresher for the bigger things I would be facing. *Simply stated:* If you can flatten the bumps and fill in the potholes of the road on which you and your students are traveling, everyone will be in for a smoother, more enjoyable ride.

Now, I hope you realize that I couldn't possibly solve all of your classroom-related management problems in just two pages. These aren't divine words; merely my thoughts. I just felt that, if I could point out an example or two of the kinds of problems I've faced over the years and their ultimate resolution, it might act—to extend the metaphor from the previous page—as a road sign pointing you in the right direction.

Let me give you two more examples of making things manageable.

CHALLENGE	CORE ISSUE / SOLUTION
A student has either lost, or never received, the activity sheet you're working on. He is now asking you for another one.	*Two core issues: 1. Do you have extra copies? 2. Can you recall where you happened to set them down two days ago?* ▲ *Run off more copies than you need. (It's only a xerox, for goodness' sake. Run ten more. It's okay. Really.)* ▲ *After handing them out, place all extra copies in an Extra Copies box. That way, there's only one spot for him to check.*

CHALLENGE	CORE ISSUE / SOLUTION
You are working with a small group. Another student approaches your table with a question or concern.	*Core issue: Although you don't like to be interrupted, the child might have a serious need.* ▲ *My students would write their name and concern on a post-it and place it on the edge of the table where I was working. Not only was the need being expressed but I was able to decide whether or not it required immediate attention.*

Solve It

So what's buggin' you? (And, no, I don't mean your students.) What little thing is causing you stress? It doesn't have to be a big thing, as you witnessed by the key story. In fact, it might be better for you to start with a small one. Small problems, as you saw in the examples above, are usually a bit easier to fix than the big ones.

Maybe you should start a little fix-it list and begin to solve some of those things that have been producing repetitive frustration. *Reality:* In order for your classroom to be a manageable place in which to live, you're going to need to sand off the rough edges.

What I've Learned

Whenever something was causing what seemed like an inordinate amount of stress, I learned to come up with a procedure for dealing with it. If not, the frustration would continue to build until I eventually reached a "snap moment."

Core Principle 6

Your students are problem solvers.

The last class I ever taught was a great one. There were so many positive, hard-working students that it made it easier for me to deal with the three or four knuckleheads in the room. (Honestly, I always had a special place in my heart for those students who were out-of-bounds more often than not. Maybe they reminded me of me when I was that age. Or maybe it was just the comic relief they injected into our days.)

Anyway, one of these students approached me one day with a lost and forlorn look.

> PITIFUL BOY
> Needin' some help:
> > *I don't have a pencil.*

Before I continue, you need to know something. It was the first week of June when he made this request.

> *Background info:* I was doing a job-share at the time. My partner, JoAnn, taught September and October, and I came in for November and December. Our students then had a month off for winter break—we were a Title I school on a year-round schedule—after which JoAnn came back for the entire second trimester. They then had another month off for spring break. For the third trimester, "Dad was home." I had them for the remainder of the school year which was set to end on July 21.

So it wasn't as if we had just started the year. We're talkin' June. But still, there he was with his pencil problem looking for help. And there I was with an unusual response.

> MR. MORRIS
> From completely out of left field:
> > *That's a problem.*
> A pause to watch Pitiful Boy's perplexed reaction and then:
> > *What's the solution?*

I wish I had a 15-second video clip to play for you so that you could see what I saw: part confusion, part disbelief, followed by a bit of thinking, and, finally, a hesitant response.

> PITIFUL BOY
> > *Borrow one?*

> MR. MORRIS
> With a big smile:
> > *Hey, good choice!*

And off he wandered to borrow a pencil.

Teacher Welfare

One of the reasons he had come to me in the first place was that he'd been conditioned to. Adults solve problems. It's true at school and true at home. Seeking adult help is what they've always done and will continue to do until they've been reconditioned.

> The other reason he came to me was due to our relationship. I had been there in the past to help him through some of his trials and tribulations, and he knew he could approach me about almost anything.

So he came to me with his problem and I decided, out of the blue, to help him solve a different problem: his utter reliance on someone else to fix things.

By not responding in a quick and easy fashion ("Here you go. I have an extra one.") or in an Old School way ("WHO DO YOU THINK I AM, THE PENCIL FAIRY?") I put the ball back in his court where it actually belonged. And by doing that, I was giving him a chance to help himself.

Student Usage

What was really great to see was how quickly my students picked up on that language. In fact, two weeks later, at a small group meeting, a student told me that he had left his assignment at home. Another student chimed in with, "That's a problem. What's the solution?" At which point the first student said, "Can I bring it in tomorrow?"

FIG. 1-2
You can find them in the products section of the New Management website.

Problem Solving Tools

Sometimes students just need the proper tool to solve a problem. And one of the truly versatile tools in our classroom was Binder Stand: a piece of plastic that turns a standard 3-ring binder into a display binder.

By placing classroom information in sheet protectors, my students no longer had to ask, "Which Book Club am I in?" They knew they could find out by flipping through the bright red Class Info binder.

It's Not Just About the Classroom

The ability to solve problems is a life-long gift you can give your students if you just show them how it's done. Sometimes it's merely a matter of identifying the core issue that is causing the problem. Other times it's making sure they have the tools they need. An important piece of the puzzle, though, is that you get out of their way so they have a chance to give their problem-solving muscles a workout.[†]

---

† The #2 reason people get fired from their jobs is that they can't get along with their co-workers. Gee, I wonder where that started? I'm guessing school. These poor people spent years in classrooms run by adults who solved most of the problems for them, which meant they were never given a chance to solve them on their own. (And in case you're wondering, the #1 reason for getting fired is absenteeism or tardiness.)

In Closing

As I mentioned at the beginning of this chapter, time and pages did not allow for a complete and thorough analysis of each of the principles. But I'm guessing that you were able to glean enough from each of them that you now have a clearer understanding of what each one means.

If that's not the case, you can always send me an email. Although I'm on the road a lot and can't always get back to you right away, I don't mind answering questions.

You can email me at rick@newmanagement.com or tweet @HappyProductive.

Margin Icons

As I did in the 2010 edition of the *New Management Handbook,* I'll place a numbered apple icon in the margin whenever the passage reflects one the six Core Principles.

To help keep things manageable, you might want to bookmark this page as a reference for when you come upon an apple later on.

Hey, look at that. We've already referred to one of them. That didn't take long.

Core Principles

YOU HAVE SAFE RELATIONSHIPS WITH YOUR STUDENTS.

YOUR WORDS EQUAL YOUR ACTIONS.

YOU ARE FAIR, FIRM, AND CONSISTENT.

YOU CAN FOCUS YOUR ATTENTION.

YOUR CLASSROOM IS MANAGEABLE FOR EVERYONE.

YOUR STUDENTS ARE PROBLEM SOLVERS.

Chapter Two

Core Principles

Confessions of a Former Echoer

The Top Ten Things I Said

Using Music for
Student Independence

Sentence Strips
Cut-and-Paste Paragraphs

Homework Made Easier

Behavior CODES

Credit Cards

An effective teacher:
Insight into soul-action,
ability to discriminate
the genuine from the sham,
and capacity to further one
and discourage the other.

—John Dewey

Chapter 2
Confessions of a Former Echoer

◆ ◆

Goals for this chapter:

☑ Understand the concept of echoing.

☑ Find out why echoing is thought to be an effective strategy.

☑ Discover the hidden dangers of echoing.

☑ Learn a simple procedure to replace your own echoing that will have your students listening better and speaking more clearly.

◆ ◆

Let me tell you about a bad thing at which I used to be really good: echoing.

Echoing—for those of you who may not know—is the Old School tradition in which teachers repeat what their students say. The practice of echoing has been around for as long as I can remember and has become, through teacher training, professional development, and repetitive use, an accepted component of classroom dialogues.

My own experience with echoing, other than the subliminal conditioning I received as a student, began early in my career. At the beginning of my second year of teaching, I volunteered to participate in a training program based upon Good and Brophy's seminal study, *Equal Opportunities in the Classroom*.

Good and Brophy were two guys who conducted some research in the late 60's that indicated teachers were not fair in how they interacted with their students. There was, they found, a pronounced bias which favored the high achievers at the expense of the low achievers. They were able to identify three different categories, or strands, in which this inequity was manifested. Each strand consisted of five sub-units. Do the math, and you'll realize they documented fifteen different ways in which teachers weren't being fair to all of their students.

The training program I was in dealt with one sub-unit every two weeks in attempt to help us overcome the bias demonstrated in the study. After winter break that year we turned our attention to Strand #2: Teacher Feedback. Our focus was on the research that indicated teachers echoed more for high achievers than they did for low achievers.

The motivation for echoing, we learned, was two-fold.

> **By repeating what a student had just said, the teacher:**
> 1) validated and confirmed what had just been shared, and,
> 2) ensured that the comments shared by the softly speaking students were loud enough to be heard by students in the back of the room.

And so, for the next two weeks in my classroom, I made a concerted effort to echo for every student.

MR. MORRIS, ROOKIE TEACHER
  Addressing the class:
    What are the three things plants need in order to grow?
  Seeing the raised hand of a student:
    Yes?

STUDENT 1
    Water?

MR. MORRIS
  Thrilled by the opportunity to echo:
    Water! That's right! I'm glad you knew that. You must know a lot about plants. Now then, what else do they need besides water?
  Seeing several students with a raised hand and calling upon one:
    Yes?

STUDENT 2
    Plants need sunlight.

MR. MORRIS
  Realizing that this echoing thing was going to be easier than he thought:
    Plants need sunlight! Yes! Sunlight is very important for plants as they grow. Good job! Now then, who knows the third one?

You can imagine the rest.

Fast forward to year fourteen of my career. There I was, somewhat weary from all of the talking. Not only was I sharing my own thoughts, but I was also repeating what the students said. End product? Verbal overload. Adding to my fatigue was the sad realization that I was doing most of the thinking and analysis during our interactions.

My over-used voice—in conjunction with my always verbalized reasoning—had created a classroom culture in which the students were checking out of the lessons and making me do most of the heavy lifting.

So, anyway, I got to thinking that maybe one way I could cut back on my verbal dominance would be to stop repeating what the students were saying.

> *Important factor:* A lot of my success in the classroom was based upon the fact that I didn't always do things the way they had always been done. I was willing to get off of the well-worn path and do a bit of exploring. This wandering led to some wonderful discoveries: the effectiveness of sign language in the classroom being one such discovery.

So I decided to stop echoing. Cold Turkey. I just quit.[†] (Poll your own students. I don't think they'll mind if they don't hear from you quite so much.)

MR. MORRIS

Addressing his students at the beginning of a new school year:

I'd like to try a new idea this year. It has to do with me not repeating what you guys say.

Pausing briefly for the thought to sink in:

I do enough talking as it is without repeating what everyone else is saying. So this year I'm going to work at not repeating words that have already been spoken. I'm also going to work at keeping my responses as short and simple as possible.

The benefits from not echoing were immediate, significant, and gratifying.

power
love
fun
freedom
safety

After an initial adjustment period, they adapted quite well. They began to enjoy the opportunity to speak more without triggering a return volley of words from their teacher. And although it took a while for me to break my reflexive echo habit, it soon became natural to just nod my head or offer a word of acknowledgment to student responses.

The benefits from not echoing were immediate, significant, and gratifying.

Benefit One

By not echoing, I no longer had to spend any stressful time trying to think of some clever, sincere comment in response to what a student had just said. That non-stop rah-rah thing had really been getting to me over the years.

---

† Believe it or not, it was much harder to stop echoing than I had anticipated. Having echoed for so many years, it had become a reflex. It actually took me a number of months to recondition myself so that I didn't automatically repeat what a student had said.

Benefit Two

By not echoing, I stopped validating right away. During all my years of echoing, I was never really aware of the fact I was embedding "yes" or "no" into almost every response. However, as soon as I stopped echoing, it became glaringly obvious. This Old School practice, I've now come to believe, can have a harmful impact on learning.

MR. MORRIS
   Doing a little informal assessment in the midst of a social studies unit:
      We've been studying the Kwakiutl Indians for a week now. Who can name a natural resource they used?

STUDENT 1
   Salmon?

MR. MORRIS
   Pleased by the validation of good teaching:
      Salmon! Yes, that's correct. Salmon was their main food source.
   Writing the word 'salmon' on the whiteboard and looking for another response:
      What other resources did they use?

STUDENT 2
   Timidly:
      Buffalo?

MR. MORRIS
   Trying not to let a bit of frustration creep into his voice:
      Buffalo? No, no, no. That was used by the other group we studied, the Cheyenne Indians. No, we're talking about the Kwakiutl who lived in the Pacific Northwest. Remember?

Life was good when the answer was "yes." But how does the teacher make "no" palatable? I'm thinking mainly about the underachievers, the fringe students, the disenfranchised. If these students were to get the feeling that their teacher was going to judge everything they said, they wouldn't say anything for fear of rejection. This would ultimately create a situation in which only the overachievers respond and the underachievers sit and watch.

power
love
fun
freedom
safety

Since it was my job to teach all of the students in my room, I felt I needed a way to make it safe for everyone to respond. This is why I began to respond with a simple, "Thanks." Thus, instead of saying "yes" to Student 1 and "no" to Student 2 as I did in the example above, I would have said "thanks" to both of them and recorded each response.

Then, after gathering a number of responses regarding the use of natural resources by the Kwakiutls, we could have used the social studies book as a resource and been able to determine which natural resources on our list were actually used and which ones weren't.

Benefit Three

Since I was no longer saying "yes" or "no" right away, I was able to drop a bad habit. I stopped playing the Match Game. The Match Game occurs whenever a teacher poses an open-ended question and then listens for one particular response. The teacher then uses that hoped-for response to begin a lesson.

> TEACHER
> Wanting to start a lesson about covered wagons:
> *Boys and girls, what was an important tool for the pioneers as they crossed the prairie?*
> Seeing a hand raised and hoping that the student is going to say 'covered wagon':
> *Yes?*

> STUDENT 1
> *A shovel.*

> TEACHER
> Disappointed by the response:
> *Shovel? Well, a shovel is a tool, but I meant an important tool.*

Students are now figuring out that their teacher is judging answers. "Shovel" was deemed less than worthy which will inhibit responses from underachievers.

> TEACHER
> Seeing another hand up:
> *Yes?*

> STUDENT 2
> *Guns.*

> TEACHER
> Getting annoyed:
> *Guns? A gun is more of a weapon than a tool. I'm asking about an important tool.*

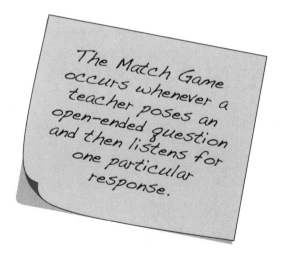

> STUDENT 3
> *Covered wagon?*

> TEACHER
> Relieved that someone finally came up with "the right answer":
> *Covered wagon! Now there you go! The covered wagon was a very important tool for the pioneers when they crossed the prairie. I'm glad you knew that.*

In these kinds of traditional dialogues, the students quickly learn that the whole question/answer thing is nothing more than a guessing game. Guess what the teacher is thinking and you'll win a brief bit of approval. The really sad thing about the Match Game is that only one student will get to be correct. It's a classic Old School mandate.

The teacher calls upon students until the correct answer is heard. The teacher then stops taking responses.

Case in Point

I arrived at a school in Los Angeles one afternoon for a presentation that was supposed to begin after they had concluded teaching for the day. Since it was a rather small staff, they decided to meet in a fifth-grade classroom. Knowing I needed to set-up my stuff ahead of time, they let me know that the teacher who taught in the room we were going to meet in was planning to take her students out for P.E. as soon as I showed up. After checking in at the office, I was led to the classroom.

FIFTH-GRADE TEACHER
    Seeing Mr. Morris enter the room:
    Oh, you're here. We'll get out of your way so that you can have the room to prepare.

MR. MORRIS
    Knowing he had a bit of time to spare:
    Not just yet. Let's play a game first, and then you can head outside.

power
love
fun
freedom
safety

So I borrowed a die from the teacher and taught her students how to play a game called "Eyeball" in which you roll the die and keep track of what number is rolled. I rolled it three times and announced the number showing each time. I then paused the game to perform a rather informal math assessment.

MR. MORRIS
    Holding up the die after the third roll:
    What is the probability of rolling a '1' on any given roll?

Reinforcing an awareness of probability was a part of why we were playing the game. The other part, of course, was to have fun. Fun, as you've already learned, is a student need.

MR. MORRIS
    Seeing about a dozen hands raised and pointing at one of the hand raisers:
    Yes?

STUDENT 1
    Not completely sure of his answer:
    1 out of 2?

power
love
fun
freedom
safety

MR. MORRIS
    Trying to keep things safe:
    Thank you.

Pointing at the next student:
Yes?

STUDENT 2
Sure of his answer:
1 out of 6!

MR. MORRIS
Knowing his response to the correct answer was going to cause a bit of confusion:
Thank you.

STUDENT 2
Somewhat shocked by not hearing words of affirmation:
[Thank you? What's up with that?]

Student 2, along with most of the class, had been conditioned to how teachers verbally respond to correct answers. Part cheerleader, part voice of authority, teachers are supposed to gush and fawn over correct answers during lessons. And since his answer was correct, he was completely disoriented when he heard me say, "Thank you."

The expression of the student sitting right behind Student 2 showed me that he, too, had been conditioned to how teachers are supposed to respond in these situations. He got a funny look on his face when I said "Thank you" to what he thought was the correct answer. I saw his up-to-then raised and waving hand slowly start to sink. It was pretty obvious to me that he thought the answer was 1 out of 6 but was confused when he didn't hear me respond to Student 2 with something along the lines of, "Yes, that's right! 1 out of 6! You must be a great math student. Blah, blah, blah."

But then he put his hand right back up, and I called on him.

STUDENT 3
Cautiously:
1 out of 5?

I thought this was a sensible adjustment to what he had thought was the correct answer. He was most likely thinking: Maybe it's not 1 compared to all of the numbers on the die but 1 compared to the other numbers.

power
love
fun
freedom
safety

MR. MORRIS
Impressed by the student's perseverance:
Thank you.

I called on ten to twelve students. Only once did we hear the correct answer.

Now, here's the trap: Had I stopped taking responses after Student 2, I would have ended up with a false assessment of their knowledge of probability, which would have greatly affected my interaction with those students. By asking and asking and asking—and making it safe to respond—I was able to gather a lot of info.

> *Formative assessment:* They've been telling us for years that assessment drives instruction. I agree. However, assessment isn't always a written thing; it's just information gathering, which I was able to do with multiple responses.

Mr. Morris
Having heard from a number of students:
I appreciate your responses to the question. And you know what? We did hear the correct answer. The correct answer is 1 out of 6. Let me show why it's 1 out of 6.

I then presented a very simple lesson on probability with a die that was more focused on the math concept than the one student who happened to know the answer.

Mr. Morris
Wanting to reinforce the learning:
What's the probability of rolling a 4 on any given roll?

I then heard:

1 out of 6
4 out of 6
1 out of 6
1 out of 6
1 out of 6

Mr. Morris
Ready to move back to the game:
If you said or thought, '1 out of 6', you are correct.

With this interaction in mind, let's improve the previous dialogue about the pioneers and the covered wagon. This time, though, we're not going to play the Match Game.

Mr. Morris
Wanting to do a little pre-assessment of the knowledge base of his students:
What was an important tool used by the pioneers as they crossed the prairie on the way to Oregon?

Student 1
The covered wagon?

Even though this was the response I was hoping for, I learned to say, "Thank you." This enabled me to keep asking, making it safe for other students to offer their responses.

MR. MORRIS
Thank you.

STUDENT 2
Rifles.

MR. MORRIS
Thank you.

STUDENT 3
Shovels.

MR. MORRIS
Shovels?

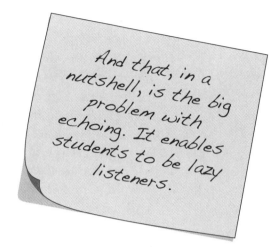

STUDENT
Yeah, shovels. For digging wagons out of the mud.

It was amazing what I heard from my students when I put more emphasis on allowing them to share their thoughts and less on what I wanted to hear. After taking several additional responses, I was able to segue to the planned lesson.

MR. MORRIS
Pleased by the responses:
You guys know a lot about the tools the pioneers used. Tell you what, let's take a closer look at one of them. Let's talk about the covered wagon.

This style of interaction enabled me to level the playing field for my students. No response was more important than another response. The students felt safe to say what they thought, and I was able to engage in an informal assessment of their general understanding of pioneer life. Not too shabby.

The Challenge of Not Echoing

The only challenge I faced by not echoing was how to deal with the handful of students who were still waiting for me to repeat what the other students were saying. And that, in a nutshell, is the big problem with echoing. It enables students to be lazy listeners.

Although students can often be fountains of knowledge during discussions, they eventually learn to tune out most comments made by classmates. It's a learned behavior. Their experience has shown them that if a student comment is important, their teacher will repeat it for everyone's benefit; thus, there's really no need to listen to other students in the first place. As you can well imagine, this subtle display of disrespect is not conducive to an effective learning environment. I think I can safely speak for all teachers when I state that students need to be attentive and truly listen to each other.

Consequently, when I observed that a number of student comments had gone unnoticed by some students, I introduced a procedure.

MR. MORRIS
In a positive but directive manner:
You know what I've noticed lately? A number of comments seem to go unheard. I'm guessing it has to do with the fact that the teachers you have had in the past have all repeated what students say. As you already know, I'm not going to do that. I also know that some of you don't speak up loudly enough. We're going to work on that this year.
A slight nodding of his head to affirm this thought before continuing:
So, from now on, when you didn't hear what another student said you should say, "echo." The student who had just spoken will then know to turn toward the source of "echo" and repeat what he had just said.

It's as simple and as complex as that. By making students accountable for what other students were saying, attentiveness and listening skills increased dramatically. And, by having the student echo his own comments, he gained the desired respect and validation.

 Granted, I'm the one who had to hold them accountable for listening. After introducing the procedure and modeling it with my students, I would then run random checks to see how well they were listening.[†]

MR. MORRIS
Nodding his thanks to a student who had just shared a great thought and then looking to the other side of the room:
Daniel, could you repeat what she just said?

DANIEL
Mounting a feeble defense:
Uh, I didn't hear her.

MR. MORRIS
Pausing for effect:
Say 'echo', please.

DANIEL
Looking in the direction of the student speaker:
Echo.

LYNDSEY
Good sport that she is:
I said.....

---

†   It should be noted that there is a difference between *hearing* and *listening*. At a staff meeting, I may be hearing the teacher who is making an announcement about something, but I am actually listening to my neighbor who is whispering to me about some funny thing that happened in her class that morning. It's the same thing with kids.

By the third week they had it down pat. And you just wouldn't believe how great it was to be in the middle of a discussion, hear a student call out "Echo," and witness the previous speaker turn and repeat what was just said. What an amazing improvement over my Old School days when I was echoing everything.

Dealing With Overuse

Prepare yourself to hear "echo!" more times than you thought possible during the first week or two of introducing this strategy. The overuse primarily stems from the novelty of the idea, and you know how students are with new ideas: they'll run 'em into the ground. By the end of the second week, though, the novelty will have worn off and things will get back to normal, or what passes for normal in your room.

power
love
fun
freedom
safety

The other factor that leads to overuse is the power students experience by being able to say "echo!" without having to ask for permission to do so. They just say it when they need to. This abuse of power issue—nothing more than human nature—will quiet down before long. Just exercise patience for the first few weeks of use.

Dealing With Abusers

If, after several weeks of use, you still have students who seem to be abusing the echo technique, call them aside and speak with them privately.

MR. MORRIS

Talking quietly with three boys in the back of the room:

Gentlemen, "echo" is a tool; it's not a weapon.

Pausing for that to sink in before continuing:

You don't need to shout it out. Just use your normal voices. We'll hear you.

Looking directly at the loudest of the three:

We always hear you.

Looking back to the other two boys:

And if we hear one "echo" from him, we don't need two more from you guys. One should do it. Also, boys, it's your responsibility to listen carefully.

Wanting to end on a positive:

power
love
fun
freedom
safety

But if you really didn't hear someone, I want you saying "echo." Let's just not go crazy with it, okay?

That was usually enough to convince the "limit testers" in my room that we were serious about using the new echo technique in the proper way. So don't be surprised when a student—or six—tries to take advantage of a new situation. It's a predictable part of how they learn to adapt and survive in their ever-changing world.

Controlled Introduction

A second grade teacher told me that she only allowed students to say "echo" during their 20 minutes of journal sharing. Within a month, "echo" had become a natural part of the sharing. What a great way to introduce a new strategy.

To try on a new idea in a limited way—think, training wheels—would help to keep it under control. Then, as the students became more skilled in its use, the teacher could slowly remove the limitations. A New Management Tip o' the Hat to that adaptation.

Saying "Echo" to the Teacher

Whenever I gave some information that a student didn't hear, there was a good chance that the child would say "echo" to me. (As I discuss in the next chapter, it's important that students feel safe whenever they ask to have something repeated.)

> Mr. Morris
>> Thinking he had everyone's attention:
>> *Your vocabulary assignment is due before lunch today.*

> Student
>> Having caught just the last few words of what Mr. Morris had said:
>> *Echo.*

> Mr. Morris
>> Calmly:
>> *Your vocabulary assignment is due before lunch today. Thanks for asking.*

power
love
fun
freedom
safety

One More Reason to Stop Echoing

Echoing does very little to improve the speaking skills of most students.[†] Students who do not speak loudly enough for everyone to hear never learn to project their voices. For them, I was really Mr. Microphone who, through the increased decibel level of my voice, could be counted on to transmit their message. What, then, was the incentive for these students to speak up? That's right; there wasn't any.

Due to my thoroughly predictable parroting, soft speakers remained soft speakers which ultimately led to: 1) a need to echo, 2) an increase in the amount of talking done by the teacher, and 3) a decrease in the listening skills of the students. The only sensible way to get off this merry-go-round was to shut it down.

Give it a Shot

You won't believe the positive change in your room if you'll only stop your echoing and encourage the students to do it for you. (Granted, it will take a bit of time for your students to adjust to the new echo philosophy; but, given time, they will adjust.) Sooner than you thought possible, you'll have a classroom full of students who not only listen to each other, but also speak in a distinct, easy-to-hear fashion.

[†]   I'm mainly referring to volume and projection. If you are working with students who have limited English proficiency, echoing and rephrasing student comments are fundamental components of language acquisition. I'm hoping, though, that as the year progresses, you can decrease the amount of echoing in which you engage, and allow the students to take over more of the modeling.

Chapter Three

Core Principles

Confessions of a Former Echoer

The Top Ten Things I Said

**Using Music for
Student Independence**

Sentence Strips
Cut-and-Paste Paragraphs

Homework Made Easier

Behavior CODES

Credit Cards

Language is a volatile truth.

—Henry David Thoreau

Chapter 3
The Top Ten Things I Said

◆ ◆

Goals for this chapter:

☑ Realize that the language you use with students has a powerful effect on their conduct.

☑ Acquire a new phrase or two that you can add to your classroom interactions.

☑ Learn to use the absence of your voice as a teaching cue.

☑ Understand that your classroom actually develops its own unique way of communicating.

◆ ◆

As I mentioned in the first chapter, quite a bit of time was spent looking back on my career as I worked on this book. Part of that reflection led to the six Core Principles, while another big chunk helped me identify a number of phrases I had used with my students, on an almost daily basis, that really helped me build an environment for success. And I'm not just talking about success for the students who were easy to teach. I'm talking about creating a classroom culture in which everyone—even the fringe students who struggle to keep their heads above water—could find an opportunity to flourish.

Students learn a great deal from our actions. (Remember Core Principle #2?) However, our words can also have a powerful effect. Here's what Haim Ginott, a noted educator and child psychologist, said about this power.

> *I've come to the frightening conclusion that I am the decisive element in the classroom. It's my personal approach that creates the climate. It's my daily mood that makes the weather. As a teacher, I possess tremendous power to make a student's life miserable or joyous. I can be a tool of torture or an instrument of inspiration. I can humiliate or humor, hurt or heal. In all situations it is my response that decides whether a crisis will be escalated or de-escalated and a student humanized or de-humanized.*

With that rather amazing and somewhat frightening statement in mind, allow me to share some of the language I used to create a happy, productive classroom.

By the way: Take their ranking, from 1 down to 10, with a grain of salt. Although that was my call, there's a good chance my students, if asked, would sort them differently.

Number 1

"Thanks for asking."

I'm not really sure *when* I developed the habit of saying, "Thanks for asking." As near as I can recall, it was around year sixteen of my career. *Why* I started to say it is a bit clearer.

"Thanks for asking" was an attempt to address my growing concern over the fact that students don't always listen carefully to what the teacher is saying.[†] Whether they are in first grade or ready to graduate from high school, it's just how their brains operate. Physiologically speaking, there's only so much information a student can receive before he has to start doing something with it. Unfortunately, though, when the student switches from information input to information processing, there will be gaps in what the student should now be receiving.

This phenomenon, to be fair, does not just pertain to students listening to teachers. It also applies to teachers listening to their principal and/or co-workers.

For instance, there were times during staff meetings when I realized that I had momentarily switched from my normal input mode to my processing mode. During the processing there would be brief periods of auditory inattention. This "attention drift" was the result of a couple of factors. One was the seemingly endless stream of words and thoughts and questions and directions and announcements that would occur during the course of the meeting. The other factor was the very real need to process all of those words and thoughts and questions and directions and announcements. (Again, it's how the brain operates.) Man, if *I* couldn't pay complete attention all the time, what was it like for *my students?*

power
love
fun
freedom
safety

So, I finally resigned myself to this sad reality: there would be times when my students listened to me the way I sometimes listened at staff meetings. As much as I'd like to think that they would hang on my every word, it just wasn't the case. Consequently, I was going to need a safe way to help my students "get back in the game" after one of those

---

† *Guesstimate:* A simple formula for calculating the length of a student's attention span, in minutes, is age + 2. Thus, an average twelve-year-old has a sustainable attention span of approximately 14 minutes.

listening gaps. Because if it wasn't safe, then a student would be less inclined to confess that he didn't know what was going on. He'd hide out, *pretend* that he knew, and quietly hope that his teacher didn't figure out that he was temporarily clueless. It's an Old School game that's been played for as long as school has been in session.

If, on the other hand, I used safe, encouraging language to welcome back the students who were trying to check in after a bit of "attention drift," then the lines of communication would stay open and students would feel secure enough to ask clarifying questions.

power
love
fun
freedom
safety

And that's why I started to use the phrase, "Thanks for asking." Although it took a bit of practice, it soon replaced the rather sharp tone that I would sometimes employ with checked-out students. It also helped foster an atmosphere of trust.

The following scenario shows this phrase in action.

"Where are we?"

Imagine that we're reading orally from our social studies book, and I'm randomly calling upon students to take a turn reading. Calvin, though, has stayed a little too long on the picture of the civil war battle. He suddenly realizes that we've moved on but doesn't know exactly where we are. He raises a hand using the sign for "I have a question."†

MR. MORRIS
   Seeing Calvin's hand:
   Question?

CALVIN
   Somewhat sheepishly:
   Where are we?

*Our sign to indicate
that the student has
a question.*

power
love
fun
freedom
safety

MR. MORRIS
   Having developed a great Inner Voice† for releasing stress:
   [Seriously? Where are we? Room 12. Where are you?]
   But knowing that he needed to be safe around his young charges:
   We're on page 88. Talking about that boldfaced vocabulary word. See it?

CALVIN
   Flipping a page, searching with his finger:
   Yeah. I got it.

MR. MORRIS
   With a smile and a nod:
   Thanks for asking.

---

† The Inner Voice is reserved for all those things you feel like saying but really shouldn't say. Unheard by students, an internal dialogue helps to release, and thus minimize, feelings of frustration and annoyance.

No rant. No rage. No sarcasm. No belittling commentary about inattentiveness.

Just a simple, "Thanks for asking."

Or, as I sometimes said just for the fun of it:

Thanks for asking. Thanks for caring. Thanks for wanting to know where we are.

What was interesting about thanking a student for asking was that I almost always got some type of acknowledgement. It wasn't usually easy to see, but it would be there if I looked for it. A little smile, a slightly nodding head as he turned to the proper page, a softly spoken "You're welcome," were all signs that told me the student appreciated my safe and respectful response to his request to have the page number repeated.

Of course, the other side of the coin is the fact that some students might take advantage of your generosity in supporting the check-in process. A student might start thinking that there's no real need to pay attention to a lesson because he can just check back in whenever he needs to by asking his teacher some type of check-in question. If this does occur, *and then continues to occur*, deal with the issue privately.

Mr. Morris
    Calling the abuser aside during an independent work time:
        Hey. It's okay to ask me what page we're on when we're taking turns reading. I have no problem with that. However, if it happens a lot, then it's not okay. It means that you're not trying very hard to be a good student.
    Pausing to make a point and then closing with something positive:
        But, trust me on this, if you really didn't know what page we're on or what math problem we're trying to solve, even though you were trying your hardest, I want you to ask. Let's just make sure that you're not taking advantage of the situation. You should be trying as hard as I am. Know what I mean?

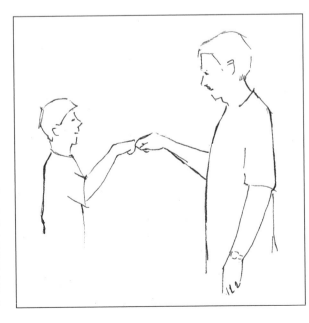

Fig. 3-1
I like to end these kinds of discussions with some type of physical contact. A hand laid gently on a shoulder, a hair tousle, or a little fist bump really helps to convey my love and concern.

Once he realized that I was serious about students paying attention and acting responsibly, he'd begin the process of self-correction. I just needed to realize that it was going to take a bit of time for him to figure out both my style of teaching and the expectations I had for my students. In the meantime, though, I worked hard to keep the whole process safe and supportive.

"What page did you say?"

Saying "Thanks for asking" was especially important to use whenever a student asked me to repeat something I had just said. It's these types of questions, though, that can really push those Old School buttons. I'm talking about a teacher who firmly believes this unwritten tenet:

The teacher should only have to announce something one time. Any student who asks to have the information repeated is also asking to be reprimanded for his apparent lack of attention.

MR. SHORTFUSE
   Already on the right page in his math guide and knowing full well the request he's about to make:
   Class, please take a look at the bar graph on page 251.

STUDENT
   Just now realizing that his teacher was addressing everyone and seeing his neighbors opening their math books:
   What page?

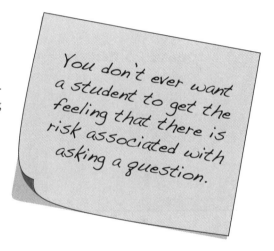

MR. SHORTFUSE
   Full of righteous indignation:
   I JUST SAID WHAT PAGE!
   WEREN'T YOU LISTENING?

Well, obviously not. That's why the student asked. But if the teacher responds in this rude and impatient Old School fashion, students learn the wrong lesson.

STUDENT
   Embarrassed by the teacher's over-reaction to his simple request:
   [Wow. That's the last time I ever ask what page we're on. It's better not knowing than getting verbally smacked down for asking.]

power
love
fun
freedom
safety

You don't ever want a student to get the feeling that there is risk associated with asking a question. This conflicts with the basic student need to feel safe in the classroom.

And so even though you might not be happy about being asked to repeat something, you shouldn't be surprised when it happens. It's just one of those predictable—and somewhat uncontrollable—occurrences that flavor our day. However, whether you respond to the request like a fire-breathing dragon or Mother Teresa is something you *can* control.

With that in mind, let's rewind that interaction and try it again.

MR. MORRIS
With his book in his hand and patience in his heart:
We're going to be looking at bar graphs today during our math lesson. In fact, take a look at the bar graph on page 251.

STUDENT
Just now realizing that his teacher had been addressing everyone and seeing his neighbors opening their math books:
What page?

MR. MORRIS
With a smile:
Page 251, please. We're going to take a look at the bar graph on that page.
After a brief pause:
Thanks for asking.

Questions That Have Already Been Answered

A rock in the shoe of many educators is the student who asks a question that was just asked and answered. Similar to the previous example, it can be a pain. But, again, it is what it is. Here's a refresher on the calming technique at the bottom of page 4.

> *Visualize parents:* One surefire way to maintain your cool and keep yourself safe is to visualize the parents of your students in the room with you. This is one of those times to do that. It will remind you to suppress your emotion-driven response and employ a more professional one.

CHECKED-OUT STUDENT
About to ask a question that has already been answered:
What do we do when we finish?

MR. MORRIS
Picturing the student's parents standing behind the student:
Would someone care to answer that?

ATTENTIVE STUDENT
Trying hard to control his annoyance:
Put your paper in the folder, mark off your number on the Check Off List,[†] and then read independently.

MR. MORRIS
With a smile:
Well said.
Turning back to the first student and again pausing briefly:
Got it?

---

†   The Check Off List is one of the management tools described in the *New Management Handbook*. It's just a half-sheet of paper with student numbers printed on it. A student draws a line through his number to indicate that he has completed an assignment.

CHECKED-OUT STUDENT
Yeah.

MR. MORRIS
With a nod of his head:
Thanks for asking.

power
love
fun
freedom
safety

Bottom line: Punctuating responses to student questions with the simple words "Thanks for asking," is a safe and loving gesture on your part that actually produces a growing desire on their part to ask questions and stay involved in lessons and discussions.

Number 2

"Calm down."

I should have had a T-shirt made with "Calm Down" printed on it. Then I could have pointed to the words instead of having to actually say them a dozen times a day.

"Calm down" is a wonderful phrase. It has the power to defuse a situation and put it in your control. It's a great phrase for all of those times, too numerous to mention let alone contemplate, when students overreacted to a situation. Either they got too emotional about something or laughed louder than was appropriate at a silly comment or joke I had just made. Regardless of which one it was, they got the same, basic response from me:

Calm down.

And if I needed to repeat it, it almost sounded like two separate sentences.

Calm.
Brief pause:
Down.

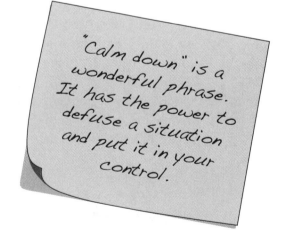

"Calm down" is a wonderful phrase. It has the power to defuse a situation and put it in your control.

And then, to emphasize the point, I didn't say a thing. I just looked around the group and did one of those, "Really?" pantomimes. You know what I mean? A subtle shake of the head, a raised eyebrow, a tilted head. Done with a light, but pointed, expression, these non-verbal signals added impact to my verbalized, "Calm down."

Then, when I had things back in control, I would proceed with what we had been doing.

power
love
fun
freedom
safety

What's Really Going On.

Students have become conditioned to exaggerate emotions in order to establish control of a situation.

> Actually, it's not just students; it's endemic throughout our society. Just watch an episode of Montel Williams or Jerry Springer. You'll witness an amazing display of the limbic, or primal/emotional, portion of the brain totally dominating the neo-cortex, or conceptual/rational, portion of the brain. It's a loud, out-of-control brawl almost completely devoid of any level-headed thinking or reasoning.

When faced with an unpleasant reality at home—doing homework, not being allowed to continue to play a video game, having to go to bed, etc.—children have learned to jack up the emotion. This not only clouds the issue being contested but also begins to wear on the parents. And if a parent does raise the white flag of surrender instead of correcting the misbehavior that led to the emotional assault, the child learns the wrong lesson.

LITTLE MONTEL
    Continuing to play his video game even though he had been asked to stop:
        [*Wow. Throwing a fit worked. I'll have to remember that.*]

The predictable outcome to this type of conditioning is that children try to apply the same tactics in class. Teachers who bow to these kinds of dramatic onslaughts merely reinforce the conditioning. Result? The emotional blackmailing continues unabated.

To counteract the harmful effects of an inappropriate emotional response, we need to teach students to control their feelings. Bear in mind, though, that you are going to have to overcome years of conditioning from the home front. As I mentioned in the introduction to the book, your students did not get the way they are overnight; thus, you can't fix things overnight. It's going to take some time, but it can be done. (Eyes on the horizon.)

A good way to begin the reconditioning is to use the phrase, "Calm down." Or, if you're working on being a more polite and respectful teacher—which is recommended with the use of Phrase #5—you could say, "Calm down, please."

MR. MORRIS
    Anticipating an over-reaction:
        I've got a new math game I want to show you.

SEVERAL STUDENTS
    Some getting up, some turning to their neighbors, some blurting out:
        Yah!
        All right!
        A GAME!
        How do you play?

MR. MORRIS
Pausing a bit for the nonsense to cease and then proceeding in a normal voice:
Calm down.
Another pause.
It's just a game.
Another pause.
I'm going to teach you how to play. Hold your questions until I have finished giving the directions.

LOUD STUDENT
Without being called upon:
We played math games last year!

MR. MORRIS
Giving a pointed look to this student:
Calm.
Pause.
Down.
Pause.
Thank you.

That comment was off-topic.

Note: An equally effective way to deal with Loud Student would be to use the sign for "that comment was off-topic." This sign, explained on page 76, would have replaced the words I used, kept me calm, and sent the same basic message.

"Calm down" is an ideal phrase to use when two students are arguing over something. This is a situation in which the emotions can really get out of control.

STUDENT 1
Approaching Mr. Morris with Student 2 following closely behind:
Mr. Morris, she took my pencil!

And before I could say a thing, Student 2 jumped in.

STUDENT 2
Loudly:
No, I didn't! He's lying!

MR. MORRIS
Before it gets any crazier:
Calm down.

STUDENT 1
Getting louder:
But she took my pencil!

MR. MORRIS
Setting an example of calmness:
I said, 'calm down.'

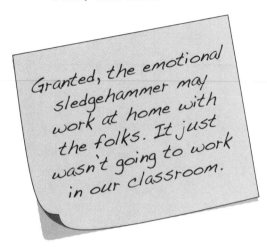

Granted, the emotional sledgehammer may work at home with the folks. It just wasn't going to work in our classroom.

Once students realized that there was no shaking Mr. Morris, that he wouldn't crack under the emotional pressure—and it sometimes took a month or so for them to figure it out—they began to adjust their behavior. Granted, the emotional sledgehammer may work at home with the folks. It just wasn't going to work in our classroom. This was an important lesson to be learned and the "Calm down" phrase helped me to teach it.

What to do when a student starts to wind it up:

> Put your Inner Voice on standby.
> Picture the parents in the room with you.
> Keep yourself calm and patient.
> Refrain from unnecessary statements.
> Avoid a rush to judgement.
> Tell the child to "Calm down."
> Give the child a moment to calm down.
> Remind yourself to "Calm down."
> Repeat as necessary.

power
love
fun
freedom
safety

Reality: In the classroom, situations can spiral out of control when emotion takes over. I'm not saying that we should all be soulless automatons. It's merely that exaggerated emotions can cloud rational interaction and adversely affect both the critical need for safety and the relationships you are trying to build with your students.

Number 3

"Good choice."

These two words perfectly summarize everything I wanted to convey to a student who had just made an appropriate decision.

STUDENT
Approaching his teacher:
Hey, Mr. Morris. I finished my assignment.

MR. MORRIS
>   *Way to go.*

STUDENT
>   *I thought I'd help Angela finish hers. She's stuck on a couple of the problems.*

MR. MORRIS
>   *Good choice. Thanks for helping.*

It was a simple declaration of appreciation and support that was easy to say, sent a clear message, and really helped to build those critical teacher/student relationships.

It's Easy to Say

I never liked to waste words.[†] What I strived for was the quality of the words I used as opposed to their quantity. In an attempt to achieve this, I found that I was constantly self-monitoring the amount of talking in which I engaged. Too much talking was counter-productive. Case in point, the statement shown below.

TEACHER
> Wanting to reinforce appropriate behavior:
>> *Class, I really like the way that Brian is working on his assignment. He's not talking to his neighbors or anything like that. He's just working hard to get his assignment done. That's really great, Brian. I wish more of our students were working the way you are right now.*

I don't know. Maybe it's just me, but I've always found monologues such as this one to be a bit patronizing. I'm also concerned about the possibility that the other students might begin to express a bit of resentment toward Brian because of these statements.

That's not to say that praise shouldn't be expressed. I'm merely suggesting it might be better if the words were directed to the student who had merited the praise.

MR. MORRIS
> Seeing Brian's on-task behavior and wanting to recognize it:
>> *Brian.*
> Waiting for Brian's attention:
>> *Look at you staying on task. Good choice, young man.*

I would have then punctuated the comment with a wink, a smile, or a nod. *Benefits:* Fewer words were used, and the words were delivered to the deserving student. And even though I hadn't made an effort to broadcast my message to Brian, I can almost guarantee that it wouldn't have gone unnoticed by the majority of my students.

---

† Research has shown that 80% of the talking done during the school day is done by the teacher. I don't think I'm going out on much of a limb if I postulate that the attentiveness of most students is going to take a beating if we serve up too much "teacher talk." How could it not?

It Sends a Clear Message

The message that "good choice" sends to students is an important one. It reflects on their sense of responsibility and self-determination, two critical cornerstones of a successful life.

Here's just one way that the message could be verbalized.

There are many things you could have chosen to do
in the situation you were facing. Some of those things were
good, some were not so good, and some were just flat-out
wrong. But you know what? From all of those options
you were facing, you chose a good one. Way to go.

To be able to express all of that in just two words makes it a statement worth using.

It Really Helps to Build Those Critical Teacher/Student Relationships

In a fundamental way, expressing your appreciation for a student's good choice enhances the relationship you have with that student. In a sense, "good choice" is a verbal pat-on-the-back; an opportunity to focus on the positive.

As opposed to the rather unfocused teacher statement from the previous page, "good choice" is directed to an individual student. And because the use of the phrase is not limited to just academic situations, I was able to use these words with my underachievers.

Student
  Approaching Mr. Morris on the playground at recess:
  Mr. Morris, Tony took the ball from me.

Mr. Morris
  I'm sorry to hear that. What did you do about it?

Student
  I asked him to give it back to me.

Mr. Morris
  With a hand placed gently on his shoulder:
  Good choice. What do you say we go see Tony and find out what's going on?

Preactive† Use of the Statement

You can use "Good choice" to help shape a positive learning environment, and as a result, not have to do so much corrective work later when things are headin' south.

---

† I've never really understood the use of the word "proactive" as a way to describe a preventative intervention. If it's really supposed to be used to indicate a preceding action, wouldn't "preactive" be a more accurate word?

MR. MORRIS
Addressing his students at the conclusion of recess before they return to the room:
Here's a good choice. When you get to the classroom, find your independent reading book and begin to read. That would be a good choice.

Although it's a bit like the teacher broadcast about Brian's work skills from the earlier example, I'm not using a student as the focal point. Instead, I'm using the appropriate behavior as a fulcrum to lift the entire class.

Number 4

"You must have thought I was kidding."

This is a funny-sounding phrase. It's not meant to be rude or disrespectful, although it may appear that way at first glance. It was just something I said to remind my students that I was serious about what I had just said, even though I had used a calm voice.

Let me back up for a second.

I used to raise my voice in the classroom. Not a lot, mind you, but enough. The times I found myself yelling were the times when I felt that my students were ignoring me because I had addressed them with my normal voice.

MR. MORRIS
Trying to get his wandering students to have a seat:
Have a seat, please.

Some students sat while others ignored the request.

MR. MORRIS
Annoyed by the disrespect and wanting to show that he was serious:
I SAID SIT DOWN! RIGHT NOW! AND I MEAN EVERYONE!

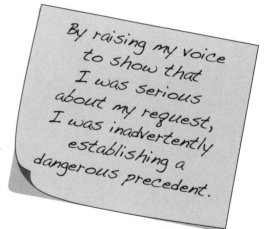

By raising my voice to show that I was serious about my request, I was inadvertently establishing a dangerous precedent.

Lo and behold, they all scurried to their seats.

Nice job, Mr. Morris. You were able to get your students to return to their seats and sit down. But at what cost?

A pretty high cost, I eventually learned. By raising my voice to show that I was serious about my request, I was inadvertently establishing a dangerous precedent.

*You can tell when Mr. Morris is serious
about something because he will yell.*

What this meant, of course, was that I would have to continue to raise my voice to convince my students I was serious. This would not have been a good way to go through the school year. But since I was relatively young and inexperienced, I hadn't yet developed the ability to employ simple actions to deal with students who were not complying with my stated expectations.

Adding to the whole mess was the fact that the students *had* taken their seats after I raised my voice. Thus, I learned that yelling works. So I continued to raise my voice whenever necessary, which conditioned my students to ignore my normal voice, which caused me to have to raise my voice. And around and around and around we went. It's something we've all experienced in one form or another as either the *yeller* or the *yellee*.

The raised-voice-means-you're-serious syndrome is so woven into the fabric of our society that it even appears in print.

Case in Point

I was reading USA Today a while back and came upon an article about obesity written by Nanci Hellmich. She started the article by stating that obesity begins in the home. This, apparently, was the conclusion drawn by nutrition experts who had been studying childhood weight issues. The group discovered that most overweight children had overweight mothers or fathers. Therefore, parents needed to be good role models when it came to making food choices.

To bolster this position, she alluded to Keith Ayoob, a registered dietian at the Albert Einstein College of Medicine in New York. Ayoob said that he had yet to meet a child who ate better than his parents did. And then he made the following statement:

```
Parents are, hands down, the biggest influence on
  their kids. They need to be good role models. I
heard a quote that said, 'What you say will speak
  to your kids. What you do will scream at them.'
```

I wholeheartedly agree with the concept that what you *do* sends a more powerful message than what you *say*. Sadly, though, our culture seems to have wholeheartedly embraced the concept that a raised voice is an indicator of intensity. Stated simply:

```
Speaking to children does not convey the same
  message that screaming at them does. Screaming
shows them that you are serious about an issue.
```

It's just one more example of how our students have been conditioned. But that's okay because, if they've been conditioned to a flawed interactive model, it also means that they can be reconditioned to respond to a more effective one.

"Did you think I was kidding?"

power
love
fun
freedom
safety

Rather than yelling or raising my voice, it would have been better for everyone involved if I had kept my voice calm. Any students who were waiting to hear the raised voice before they complied would had received a private reminder about how I operated.

> MR. MORRIS
> Using his dog squeak toy to signal, "Stop, look, listen" to his students:
> *Squeak, squeak, squeak.*

(It doesn't really sound like that, but you can use your imagination.)

After generating a few squeaks, though, I noticed that two students did not stop, look, and listen. I wrote down their names as a reminder to speak with them later and then focused my attention on the twenty-nine students who did comply.

> MR. MORRIS
> Calmly:
> *You guys worked so hard in your groups just now that we were able to finish a bit early. Tell you what, let's work on seat covers for the next ten minutes.*[†]

I set a digital timer for ten minutes so that I wouldn't have to keep an eye on the clock and then called over the two students who had not done a very good job of responding to the dog squeak toy.[††]

> MR. MORRIS
> Calmly:
> *Thomas and Dylan.*

Dylan's head popped up.

> MR. MORRIS
> Directing his voice to Thomas:
> *Thomas.*

A student poked Thomas. He looked up.

> MR. MORRIS
> With a smile:
> *May I have a word with you two?*

[†]   The Seat Cover project teaching guide can be downloaded from the website. (newmanagement.com)
[††]   The use of timers and sound makers is described in Lesson 5 of the *New Management Handbook*.

Thomas and Dylan drew close.

> MR. MORRIS
> Showing them the squeak toy:
> *The sound this squeak toy makes is a signal. What does the signal mean?*

> DYLAN
> Realizing he's busted:
> *It means "Stop, look, listen."*

> MR. MORRIS
> Always looking for the positive:
> *Right you are. It means "Stop, look, listen." But you didn't. I squeaked it three times and it didn't seem to faze you two at all. You must have thought I was kidding.*

> THOMAS
> Ever the weasel:
> *Oh, no. We know you're serious.*

> MR. MORRIS
> Focused on the objective:
> *But you didn't stop. You didn't look. You didn't listen. So I'll ask you both again. Did you think I was kidding?*

Thomas and Dylan shook their heads "no" and offered a feeble assortment of excuses.

> MR. MORRIS
> Always thinking about the future:
> *You're right. I wasn't kidding. So, what are you going to do the next time you hear the squeak?*

> THOMAS AND DYLAN
> Almost in unison:
> *Stop, look, and listen.*

> MR. MORRIS
> Ending on the positive:
> *Always a good choice. Thanks, boys. Carry on.*

 And if the boys were to ignore the squeak the next time I used it, which is possible, then I would need to back up my words with actions. (See pages 6 and 7 for suggestions.)

"What don't you get?"

This was a question I sometimes posed to students when I was speaking to them privately about their non-compliance. It was a simple variation on the "you must have thought I was kidding" theme.

power
love
fun
freedom
safety

"What don't you get?" actually sounds more like, "What doncha git?" but without the Tony Soprano vibe. In fact, I said it in such a way that I actually conveyed curiosity more than anything else. And although it takes a bit of practice, you'll soon be able to say "What doncha git?" in a safe and loving manner.

It's a very focused phrase that does not allow for a lot of wiggle room. It puts the ball squarely in the child's court and cuts off a common form of student resistance: denial.

"What doncha git?" would have been ideal in the preceding example. Let me show you what I mean.

> MR. MORRIS
>> Showing them the squeak toy:
>>> *The sound this squeak toy makes means "Stop, look, listen." I squeaked it three times and it didn't seem to faze you two at all. You must have thought I was kidding.*

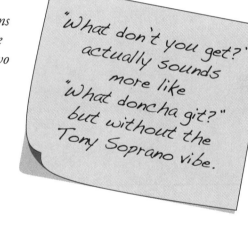

> THOMAS
>> Ever the weasel:
>>> *Oh, no. We know you're serious.*

> MR. MORRIS
>> Focused on the objective:
>>> *But you didn't stop. You didn't look. You didn't listen.*
>> Pausing slightly before continuing:
>>> *What doncha git?*

What could they have possibly said at this point? Well, one of two things actually. They may have responded with "We get it" or possibly some mumbled statement of confusion regarding the procedure we were discussing.[†] Regardless of the response, I would have been able to handle it effectively.

If they had said, "We get it," then I could have addressed their somewhat appalling lack of respect for our procedures.

> MR. MORRIS
>> With a puzzled look:
>>> *So you understand what the squeak toy means but you're not doing what you're sup-*

---

†   If they were to try to lead the discussion astray with any number of denial strategies—a classic student ploy—I'd bring them back to reality with a simple, "We're not talking about that right now. I asked you what you didn't get about the dog squeak toy meaning stop, look, listen?"

posed to do. That sounds to me as if you two gentlemen just don't care about following our procedures.

THE BOYS
Shocked by the implications:
Oh, no. We care.

MR. MORRIS
Calmly:
Saying you understand and showing you understand are two different things.

And we were right back to our "What are you going to do the next time you hear the squeak toy?" line of questioning.

If, instead, they had said that they weren't clear about the procedure—which happened in the beginning—then I could have provided them with a brief review.

power
love
fun
freedom
safety

MR. MORRIS
Attempting to remain a patient and loving teacher:
Stop whatever it is you are doing. Stop without any delay. Don't try to finish some task. Don't think you have to return to your seat. Just stop.
A nod of the head to punctuate step one and then:
Look my way. When you are actually looking at me, it will be easier for you to concentrate on what I am saying.
Another nod, a brief pause, and then:
Listen. Listen carefully. And please ask if you are unsure about what I'm saying.
Bringing it all home:
Boys, I'll expect to see a better job the next time you hear the squeak toy. Back on task, please.

Delivered in a non-emotional fashion, the boys would have now realized that I was serious about our procedures. And, as mentioned earlier, if they were again remiss at complying, I would have probably stepped it up a notch with a "When....then" statement. (See page 7 for a refresher.)

Number 5

"Please."

I'm pretty sure we can all agree on the fact that teachers are the primary role models for their students when it comes to politeness and civil behavior. In a sense, you reap what you sow. If you're not polite with your students, you're not going to see them being polite with you or their classmates.

That's why the dialogue with Dylan and Thomas ended with the word, "please." Not only will this simple word take the edge off of almost any directive, it will also elevate the level of interaction by demonstrating a clearly stated respect for the students and their need to be treated with dignity.

Teachers are sometimes more concerned with getting respect than they are with giving it. Respect, though, is a two-way street. And two-way streets, as we already know, are supposed to have traffic flowing in both directions.

To avoid gridlock, you might want to develop the habit of verbalizing all kinds of courtesy and respect.

> When a student does something that you appreciate:
> *Thank you.*

> When a student thanks you:
> *You're welcome.*

> When a student sneezes:
> *Bless you.*

Try it. I think you'll like it.

Respect, though, is a two-way street. And two-way streets, as we already know, are supposed to have traffic flowing in both directions.

Number 6

"What are you doing?"

"What should you be doing?"

"What are you going to do now?"

Bargain day. You get three phrases for the price of one. These three questions form the basis of a Glasser dialogue I used for years. It provided me with the information I needed in order to make a decision about situations that occured in the classroom. Without the necessary information, I ended up making decisions based upon my assumption about what was going on. And since my assumptions varied from one student to the next, I sometimes ended up putting my foot firmly in my mouth.

Redirecting Off-Task Behavior

Imagine that my students were working independently on a math assignment. I looked at Max, the name for our trusty digital timer, and saw that we had four minutes left in which to complete it. I then looked up and noticed that Nicole was doing nothing. My assumption: *Nicole is one of my best math students. Therefore, I'm guessing she finished early and will be moving on to something else.*

I then looked over and saw Calvin doing nothing. Sadly, I had a whole different set of assumptions for him than I did for Nicole.

OLD SCHOOL MR. MORRIS
  Without really knowing what was going on:
  HEY! HOW COME YOU'RE NOT WORKING ON YOUR MATH!

CALVIN
  Feeling a bit indignant:
  *I FINISHED MY MATH. I WAS JUST ABOUT TO WORK ON MY
  JOURNAL. WHY ARE YOU ALWAYS PICKING ON ME?*

Had I merely asked what he was doing, Calvin would have answered, "I finished my math. I'm working on my journal." I would have then been able to say, "good choice." But I didn't ask and thereby lost an opportunity to improve our relationship. Sigh.

Step 1: "What are you doing?"

To avoid a rush to judgement, I learned to take a moment and find out what was really going on.

MR. MORRIS
  Seeing Calvin doing nothing and approaching his desk:
  What are you doing?

Now then, if Calvin were indeed off-task when questioned, there was a good chance he would not provide a verbal response. Instead, he would suddenly engage himself in the independent math assignment and hope that his change in behavior would be enough to deflect the question and the questioner. Nice try, but no.

MR. MORRIS
  Not getting a verbal response from Calvin:
  Calvin. Talk to me. What were you doing when I walked up to your desk?

I wanted to hear him say, "Nothing." In order to help him improve his behavior, he needed to be made aware of what was getting in his way. And in this situation, being off-task was getting in the way of Calvin becoming a better student.

CALVIN
  Reluctantly:
  Nothin'.

Step 2: "What should you be doing?"

To be fair, it was possible–not likely, but within the realm of possibility–that he didn't know what he should have been doing. Maybe he had just gotten back from working with the resource teacher. Maybe he had just returned to school from a dental appointment. Maybe, just maybe, he had finished the math assignment and was basking in the glow of the moment while trying to figure out what to do next.

MR. MORRIS
Patiently:
What should you be doing?

CALVIN
Realizing that further resistance is futile:
My math.

Step 3: "What are you going to do now?"
This third question, I now realize, was actually a MacKenzie-type question.[†] It's a transfer-of-ownership question. It's a question which required the student to become involved in the decision-making process.

> *Bonus:* "What are you going to do now?" had the additional benefit of providing an opportunity for the student to engage in a bit of face-saving, i.e., he would be the one to get himself back on-task and not the teacher. You always want to keep your eyes open for those character-building opportunities in which students can be led from the drudgery of obedience and into the bright light of self-determination.

MR. MORRIS
Firm yet safe:
What are you going to do now?

CALVIN
Looking to make the best of a bad situation:
My math.

MR. MORRIS
With a smile and a pat on the shoulder:
Good choice.

And with that, I walked away. I wouldn't need to stand over him to ensure he got back to work. I just wandered away to help someone else while keeping a casual eye on Calvin.

Not only did this dialogue help to make me a safer teacher, it also began to work in my favor as time went by. Because I used the dialogue so frequently, my students were eventually able to anticipate the three questions. Consequently, it became possible to get Calvin back on-task by merely sending a puzzled look his way.

---

†   This is, of course, the same Robert MacKenzie I wrote about in Chapter 1—page 6—and the author of *Setting Limits in the Classroom.*

CALVIN
    Seeing the 'What are you doing?' look from Mr. Morris:
        [Uh, oh. Here he comes. What am I doing? What should I be doing?
        What am I going to do now?]

And without a word from me, he could have gotten himself back on task. It was the repetitive use of dialogue, though, that set the stage for him to develop his growing sense of accountability and self-determination.

Avoiding the Rush to Judgement, Take Two

I was in the classroom one day at lunchtime when some girls came into the room to hang out. Within a minute or so, they were at the whiteboard with the markers.† Since we never use the whiteboards as "toys," I felt the need to address their poor choice.

MR. MORRIS
    Girls, you know better than that.

SPOKESGIRL FOR THE GROUP
    Turning to me innocently:
        Oh, we were working on the list of names for the social committee you asked us to
        organize.

Ouch.

MR. MORRIS
    Pausing long enough to remove his foot from his mouth:
        Girls, I apologize. I should have asked what you were doing. Thanks for remembering
        to take care of the committee list.

Here's what I finally had to ask myself:

Question

What have I got to lose by asking?

Answer

Actually, there's nothing to lose
and everything to gain.

---

†   According to our Class Glossary—as explained in the *New Management Handbook*—the whiteboard is a tool, not a toy. Therefore, no one should be doodling on it.

Number 7

"Take a risk. You're among friends."

This phrase was created in response to the research done by Mary Budd Rowe, a science education professor at Stanford. In her ground-breaking study, *Wait Time: Slowing Down May Be a Way of Speeding Up*, she discovered that teachers move too quickly during question/answer sessions with their students.

Here's what she observed:
1. A teacher would ask a question.
2. Almost immediately, responses would be provided by overachievers.
3. An "awkward pause" would occur during which no one responded.
4. The teacher would move forward with the lesson.

Upon further review and analysis, Rowe found out that there could be huge gains in learning, understanding, and achievement if teachers were to slow down the interaction just a bit. To help bring about this gain, and improve the quantity and quality of student responses, she suggested that teachers not allow the awkward pause to deter their questioning. In fact, she came up with two simple strategies for effectively handling the pause.

Restate the Question

The first strategy was to restate the question. As I mentioned during the explanation of the "Thanks for asking" phrase, my students didn't hang on my every word and, as a consequence, I found myself restating questions constantly. Repeating a question helped to fill the pause, engaged students who may have missed the question the first time I had asked it, and sent a very powerful message to my students. The message was twofold:

We're not going anywhere.
We're still talking about this question.

Encourage Students to Respond

power
love
fun
freedom
safety

The other pause-filling strategy was to encourage students to share their thoughts. The safety students felt when they were encouraged and supported went a long way toward getting the resistant learners to express their views. Add the fact that they knew most responses received a non-judgemental "thanks" from their teacher[†] and it was win-win.

MR. MORRIS
Waiting patiently for students to respond after having restated his question:
Take a risk. You're among friends.

It amazed me to see the responses begin to flow whenever I said those six simple words.

---

† This technique, you may recall, was covered in Chapter 2: Confessions of a Former Echoer.

Professor Rowe's Findings

If teachers waited through the pause, restated the question, and encouraged students to share their thoughts, underachievers' responses went up 400%.[†]

Number 8

"Back on task, please."

In the classroom, I was all about on-task behavior. It was at the top of my list of things I looked for as I interacted with students. On-task behavior was manifested in many ways.

> Paying attention to a lesson.
> Reading independently.
> Knowing where we are in the book when we are reading orally.
> Working on an assignment.
> Working with a group on a project.

Since students sometimes drift away from what they should be doing, I realized I was going to need a simple phrase to get them back to the task at hand.

Mr. Morris
   Walking by a group who seemed to be engaged in social talk instead of the project:
      Back on task, please.

There's no morality play or lecture. No pointing finger or empty threats. Just a simple declaration of what the group needed to do.

"Back on task, please" was also a great way to punctuate an announcement I had made to the class if it had been delivered while they were working on an independent activity.

Mr. Morris
   Squeaking the dog toy to get everyone's attention:
      I'd like everyone to draw a star next to problem number 10 on your activity sheet. We're going to do that one together as a group. So, draw a star next to it and then skip over it. Any questions?
   Not a peep:
      Thanks for listening. Back on task, please.

It was an easy thing to say, sent a clear message to my students, and was a more palatable statement than the Old School, "Get back to work." The word "work" just didn't have that same uplifting quality that "on task" did. It's a little thing, I know; nonetheless, it's the slow accumulation of little things that adds up to big things.

[†]   Since your underachievers are the ones with the most potential for growth, following Rowe's advice will help to improve the overall test scores for your class.

Number 9

"Could you do a sample, please?"

This is a phrase I taught my students to use because, for the most part, they didn't always know how to ask for help. This was especially true when were in the middle of a lesson and one of them was confused about something.

CONFUSED STUDENT
I don't get it!

I had heard this quite a bit during my early years of teaching and usually responded in the same, predictable Old School way.

MR. MORRIS
What don't you get?

CONFUSED STUDENT
More confused than ever:
*[Is he asking me to explain what I don't get? Hey, if I could explain it,
I'd understand it.]*
With a touch of frustration:
I JUST DON'T GET IT!

When I eventually realized that "What don't you get?" was an ineffective response, I came up with a better way to go. I taught my students to ask for a sample. And although I explained when to use the phrase and exactly what it meant, it still took about a month or so for them to develop the habit of using it. To help them along, I took the lead.

MR. MORRIS
Seeing that some of his students were looking at their neighbors for clarification about what he had just said to everyone:
If you'd like a sample, just ask.

CONFUSED STUDENT
Could you do a sample, please?

What he was really saying was:
Hey, Mr. Morris. Stop talking. Your words are doing me no good.
Could you model what you're talking about.
Could you draw what you're talking about.
*If it's a written assignment you're asking us to do, could you show me what
it's supposed to look like?*
Could you have some students demonstrate what you're talking about?
Because if you just repeat what you already said, I'm still going to be confused.

This was the beauty of "could you do a sample, please?" It was safe language. It didn't mean the student was stupid. It didn't mean he hadn't been paying attention. It didn't mean he hadn't been trying hard. It merely meant he wanted the information to be presented in a different way than it already had already been.

MR. MORRIS
Happy to do a sample. Thanks for asking.

This will, of course, cause you to have to stretch a bit as a teacher. You'll have to learn how to present information in more than one way. But that's okay. The more you do it, the better you'll get. And the better you get at teaching, the more your students will get out of your lessons and the less they'll ask for a sample. It's the classroom version of the Circle of Life.

Number 10

Not saying anything.

If there was one big recommendation I could make to new teachers, it would be this:

Stop talking so much.

I'm not sure why teachers, especially new ones, use so many words. It could be the result of years of conditioning they received from their own teachers. Teachers have always talked a lot. It comes with the job.

I teach, therefore I talk.

A lot as it turned out. More than I should have, probably, but I didn't know a better way to go than to use my voice for just about everything.

It could be that new teachers are insecure about their ability to control the class and, in an effort to exert control, they use their voices to dominate the room. Using your voice is convenient. It's easy. That's not to say that it's effective. It's just that your voice is always handy, so why not use it?

There are several reasons actually.

One is that you would never want to use your voice so much that your students become desensitized to it. This will, as you can imagine, have a harmful effect during the course of a lesson when they need to be absorbing your words of wisdom regarding, say, the proper way to make a plural out of a noun that ends with the letter "y."

For another—and it's something that has already been addressed in Chapter 1—students don't always respond to the spoken word. This is especially true if you're trying to use your words to correct misbehavior. What students are waiting for in those situations is some kind of action to go along with all of those words.

It would be better to recondition our students to the fact that we're not always going to use our voices. That, in my opinion, would be a pleasant change for everyone involved.

From the Trenches

I was visiting the classroom of a new teacher one day. I was just there to hang out and maybe play a few classroom games. After about an hour or so of being in the room, I was somewhat saddened to see that the teacher was using his voice way too much. In fact, about half of the time he was talking about students who were interrupting the lesson he was trying to teach. Talking about not talking. How crazy is that?

WELL-MEANING TEACHER
Impatiently:
Hey. What did I say about interrupting me? You need to raise your hand if you wish to say something. Let's all remember that, okay?

At which point the interrupter would raise a hand and the teacher would then call upon him.

The result?
The student got to say what he wanted to say.

The cost?
The entire class received an Old School verbal broadside about interrupting.

The predictable outcome:
Students continued to interrupt the teacher—and one another—because the cost for interrupting was negligible.

Anyway, it came my time to introduce a game. I had barely begun to provide an explanation of the game when one of the students interrupted me.

IMPULSIVE STUDENT
Without being called upon:
Does the winner get a prize?

I didn't say a word. I just stopped my explanation in mid-sentence, turned, and looked at the student with a quizzical look. I then looked away for a moment before looking back at him. During this brief time, a rather awkward silence settled over the room. You could almost hear some of the students thinking, "Man, I'm glad *I* didn't interrupt this guy."

After waiting about four seconds beyond total silence,[†] I addressed the student.

MR. MORRIS
With a determined look:
May I continue?

STUDENT
Surprised by the patience of his request:
Oh, yeah. Sorry.

I was interrupted once more during the explanation and the interrupter received the same treatment but with an additional twist.

MR. MORRIS
Calmly addressing the class:
You know, if this game is going to cause some of you to do things you know you shouldn't do—such as interrupting someone—you probably shouldn't play. You can just sit and watch the first game if that would help.

They all got the message and the interruptions stopped. But notice how it was the absence of my voice in response to the first student—in addition to the ensuing silence—which helped to teach the lesson that his interruption was inappropriate.

As you probably know by now, I taught for thirty-one years. But here's something you may not know: The more I taught, the less I talked.

Last Thought

If the language I identified in this chapter does not match your style, substitute your own. Maybe the words, "Take a risk. You're among friends." doesn't do it for you. If that's the case, don't abandon the concept behind the phrase, just the phrase itself.

TEACHER
Encouraging students during the awkward pause:
Let's hear those great ideas I know you have.

More comfortable language for you, and the same outcome for them.

Win-Win.

[†]   Even though I had everyone's undivided attention, I still waited an additional four seconds—or so—before I addressed the student. Believe it or not, waiting four seconds added to the message I was trying to send.

Chapter Four

Core Principles

Confessions of a Former Echoer

The Top Ten Things I Said

Using Music for Student Independence

Sentence Strips
Cut-and-Paste Paragraphs

Homework Made Easier

Behavior CODES

Credit Cards

The music in my heart I bore,
Long after it was heard no more.

—William Wordsworth

Chapter 4
Using Music for Student Independence

◆ ◆

Goals for this lesson:

☑ Understand why your voice is not always the best way to communicate with your students.

☑ Be able to use a song to initiate a simple classroom procedure.

☑ Learn about the different songs on the TV Theme Songs CD.

☑ Discover how to use an iPad, iPhone, or iPod Touch as the sound system in your room.

◆ ◆

One of the most popular strategies I share during professional development presentations involves the use of TV theme songs as a way to transmit simple directions to students. Using music as a management tool not only adds a powerful new element to what is normally a voice-dominant environment, it also helps students develop self-control: something they're going to need if they are to become truly independent.

For example, whenever I played the theme to *Bill Nye, the Science Guy*,[†] my students knew to:

1. Stand up,
2. Slide their chairs under their desks, and
3. Come join me on the carpet.

This conditioned response to a simple musical cue was beneficial for many reasons.

For one, it helped reduce the amount of talking I was doing. As I mentioned in the footnote at the bottom of page 43, research has shown that 80% of the talking done during the school day is done by the teacher. If I wasn't careful, my over-used voice would have become invisible about halfway through the year. How great, though, that I was able to cut down on the number of words I spoke by allowing a short song to speak for me.

---

† Look on page 75 for information about the best website for downloading additional TV and cartoon theme songs.

Another advantage was the fact that music is a right-brain cue. This under-utilized aspect of effective communication proved to be especially significant when I needed to momentarily interrupt independent work to make an announcement.

Without any verbal input from me, the entire class, regardless of their primary language, was able to comply with simple, pre-determined directions.

The sadly pathetic verbal pleas for attention I used as a new teacher such as:

Boys and girls...   Eyes, please...   1, 2, 3...

never worked well. I found I had to jack up the volume of my voice in order to gain everyone's attention.

And then, one day, I came upon some research: 95% of assignments being completed independently by students are tasks that require significant left-brain activity. Hmmmm.

So even though it was relatively quiet because they were consumed with the activity, a left-brain cue—my spoken announcement—was going to fall on deaf ears. (If it helps, picture yourself standing out in the rain and trying to get someone's attention with a squirt gun. Not gonna work.)

Okay, then. Since the left brain was sending me a busy signal, I figured I should try communicating with the right brain. And that's what music enabled me to do. It cut through the verbal storm raging inside of each little head and delivered a clear, distinct message.

power
love
fun
freedom
safety

A final benefit to using music was that it provided opportunities for my students to develop a sense of self-determination. Without any verbal input from me, the entire class, regardless of their primary language, was able to comply with simple, pre-determined directions. These small acts of self-direction had a significant impact on the students' sense of independence and autonomy. And when they finally acquired the ability to be self-controlled, the potential for growth was without limits.

Getting Started

As is the case with most procedures, there are many important steps which must be taken so that students will respond to the music in an appropriate fashion. In other words, before your class will be able to transition from one activity to another guided solely by the melodic pacing of, say, the *Jeopardy* theme song, a framework will have to be established.

On the following pages you'll find twelve easy steps that will help you begin using music effectively in your classroom. The first five you can do yourself. Steps 6 through 12 will be done with the students. Throw in a bit of time for them to practice the routine for the first song you introduce and you should be good to go.

Steps for the Teacher

Step 1: Find a CD Player That Works†

This may seem like a silly step due to the rather startling leap forward in technology education has taken over the past ten years. Nonetheless, the thought is symbolic of one of the six Core Principles. (#5: Your Classroom Is Manageable for Everyone.) By breaking the procedure down into a series of doable actions—a process the management gurus refer to as chunking—you're increasing the likelihood that your ultimate goal will be met.

So, don't be in a rush to get to Step 7: Play the Song, when the first six steps, regardless of their seeming simplicity, may prove to be crucial components for success.

Step 2: Plug It In

Another no-brainer, right? But think about it. Where does your music player need to be located? Since it actually depends upon your equipment, I've listed eight possibilities.

1. **CD player (boom box) with remote control**
   If it's got a remote control, you can place the player in the back of the room so that the sound doesn't blast you. This also means, though, that it won't be as easy to change CD's if you need to. (You won't have to worry about this with the TV theme songs since they're all on the one CD that came with this book.)

2. **CD player without remote control**
   If your player doesn't have a remote control, you'll need to keep things close to you. This might actually be preferable at first. By having the controls at hand, you'll find it easier to access the tracks you want to use.

3. **CD player with remote control and detachable speakers**
   If you discover that musical cues are something you'd like to employ on a regular basis, you might want to consider getting a boom box with a remote control and detachable speakers. That's what I had in my room. The remote enabled me to place the player in the back of the room so that it was out of the way. The detachable speakers were placed on the top of some cabinets. This produced better sound coverage than the conventional speakers-at-the-source arrangement.

---

† CD Player is the label I'll use to cover the wide variety of musical devices available for playing songs.

4. Computer connected to speakers

If you use a computer as a teaching tool—and it's accessible, always on, and connected to speakers—you might want to consider using the computer as your music machine. How easy would it be, using iTunes, to find the song you want on your computer and give it a quick double-click? Yeah. Easy.[†]

If you have an iPad, iPhone, or iPod Touch:

5. Use computer speakers

Kaizen:
The Japanese philosophy of "continuous improvement."

With the purchase of an iPod Touch, I did a kaizen thing and took music to a whole new level. I put the songs on my iPod and connected it to some computer speakers located in the back of the room. Wow. Having all of my classroom music in one handy little package made it so much easier to play songs and control the volume. (*Tip:* I bought a 50-foot head-phone cable from Monoprice.com for a couple of bucks.)

6. Bluetooth receiver (wireless)

Speaking of computer speakers, you can connect them to a Bluetooth receiver—I found one in Brookstone for $30 that works great—and be able to wirelessly send music to the receiver which passes it along to the speakers.

7. Bluetooth speakers (wireless)

Although sometimes sketchy when it comes to making a clear connection between your device and the speakers, it's a great option. And over the past number of years, the quality of Bluetooth devices has gotten better. Just know that good Bluetooth speakers are somewhat expensive.

8. Built-in classroom speakers

If this is you, smile. All you have to do is connect your device to the plate with a simple patch cord and you'll be set to rock the house.

For right now, try to keep it simple. It's going to take living with the whole thing before you'll have your music system all dialed in and set up in a way that works for you and your students.

Note: For a more detailed explanation on how to create a classroom sound system, check out the iBook I wrote. The link to the book is on my website.

[†]   One of my personal principles for success in the classroom was this: If I could make something easier to use, I was more likely to use it. Thus, the easier it is for you to access your music, the more likely it is you'll use music as a management tool. And the bonus to music? You'll be promoting student independence.

Step 3: Select a Song

My recommendation is that you start with a short, simple song. *Bill Nye* is a good one. There are enough elements in the song that your students, within a reasonably short time, will be able to learn the song and anticipate its conclusion.

The *Jeopardy* theme song is another good choice because of the predictable nature of the piece. There are four repetitions of the melody line—each in a different key—before you get to the well-known closing notes.

If you happen to have a really challenging group of students, you might want to begin with the *Andy Griffith* theme song. It's only thirteen seconds long and would be ideal for something as simple as lining up at the door.

Step 4: Become Familiar with the Song

Play it for yourself so that you get a good feel for the music. As you listen, visualize yourself calmly watching your students as they successfully respond to the music.

Step 5: Assign a Procedure to the Song

It should probably be something pretty clear cut. For example, COME TO THE CARPET is better than ORGANIZE YOUR DESK. Come to the carpet is a yes/no kind of thing. You're either on the carpet or you aren't.

The ORGANIZE YOUR DESK issue is much more subjective and therefore will be more difficult for you to quickly assess individual compliance. This quick assessment is a significant issue. Your overall success will be partially dependent upon your ability to hold students accountable for complying with your agreed-upon procedure. Therefore, if it's easier for you to determine their compliance, then it will be easier for you to identify, and deal with, the non-compliers.

Your overall success will be partially dependent upon your ability to hold your students accountable.

If you don't normally have your students meet on the carpet, come up with something else for your students to do on a regular basis that is easily verifiable. GET OUT YOUR PLANNER is a good example. Similar to the COME TO THE CARPET procedure, GET OUT YOUR PLANNER is a yes/no type of response to a particular song.

power
love
fun
freedom
safety

Reality: Using a song to signal your students to get out their homework assignment may not seem significant at the moment. However, the cumulative effect of using six different songs to signal six different procedures will enable you—and your students—to deal with repetitive, tedious behaviors in a playful new way.

So, a quick recap of your progress to this point finds that you:

1. Have a working CD player,
2. Have plugged it in,
3. Have selected one of the songs,
4. Have become familiar with it, and
5. Have decided upon a procedure for your students.

It's now time to introduce the music/procedure concept to your students. Hey, this is easier than you thought it was going to be, huh?

Steps with the Students

Step 6: Introduce the Song

You're now ready to share your first song with your students. Make sure the CD player is ready to go, the volume is properly adjusted, and your song is cued up.

MR. MORRIS
    I'm going to play a song for you. It's called Bill Nye, the Science Guy.

SEVERAL STUDENTS
    Mumble, mumble, some blurting, some side talking, general excitement.

MR. MORRIS
    Not saying a word, just looking around the room and shaking his head ever so slightly.

Reality 101: Don't be surprised at any overreaction to your statement. Kids love music. And they love anything new. Some of them, however, will take advantage of the novelty and use it as an opportunity to release pent-up energy. If that happens, just stay calm.

MR. MORRIS
    After waiting for the buzz to go away:
    Calm down. It's just a song. Some of you might know it. Some of you might not. It doesn't really matter. I'm going to play the song and I want you to listen to it without reacting. I'll give you a chance to share your thoughts when the song is over.

Step 7: Play the Song

After a brief pause—it should be silent and you should have their attention—go ahead and play the song. If you get any kind of a loud outburst or any kind of "I know that song!" just stop the music. Don't say anything. Maybe look off to the side. Let your silence convey the message that their response was not appropriate.

> MR. MORRIS
> Waiting until it's quiet and then using a calm, patient voice:
> *Just. Listen.*

Start the song over. You should have their cooperation at this point.

Step 8: Allow a Response

power
love
fun
freedom
safety

At this point in the proceedings, they're going to want to make some type of comment or share some response to the song. You might as well go ahead and let them get it out of their systems so that you can then move on to the next step. (To handle off-topic comments, check page 76 for the sign language to use. Sign language is a better way to go than the Old School verbal scolding about keeping comments relevant.)

Step 9: Introduce the Procedure

After everyone has had a chance to share their thoughts—patience, please—introduce the procedure associated with the song.

> MR. MORRIS
> *The song we just heard, Bill Nye, the Science Guy, is going to be a special song for us. Whenever you hear this song you're going to stand up, put your chair under your desk, and come join me on the carpet. That was three different steps.*
> Going to the whiteboard and grabbing a pen:
> *What was the first step?*

> STUDENT 1
> *Stand up.*[†]

[†] There was a distinct possibility that a student or two, because of their inattention, would have stood up at this point. If this did happen, I would just stop talking and look at them with a quizzical look. If that didn't get them to sit back down, I would have used sign language. (You can check page 76 for the 'sit down' sign.) That usually took care of it. If not, I would have addressed them verbally.

> Mr. Morris
> *Have a seat, please. These steps are for when you hear the Bill Nye song.*

MR. MORRIS
Thank you.
Writing the first step on the board:
Step 1: Stand up.[†]

MR. MORRIS
Raise your hand if you remember the second step.

STUDENT 2
I think it was put your chair under your desk.

MR. MORRIS
Thank you.
Calling upon several more students and then finally acknowledging the correct response and writing it on the board:
Step 2: Slide your chair under your desk.
Turning back to the students:
And Step 3 is…
Looking for a student with a hand up.

STUDENT 3
With a nod from Mr. Morris:
Go to the carpet.

MR. MORRIS
Writing the third step on the board:
Thanks.

Step 10: Students Model the Procedure

Even though you've carefully verbalized the procedure and have even written the steps on the board, it's always a good idea to have a small group of students model it for everyone. There's nothing like a student demonstration to clear up any lingering confusion.

MR. MORRIS
We need three students to demonstrate this procedure for us.

---

†   I realize I didn't take multiple responses to these questions as described in Chapter 2: Confessions of a Former Echoer. That's because I liked to be somewhat flexible in how we interacted. Sometimes I took multiple responses; sometimes I didn't. It's just how it went.

I'd recommend choosing a top student, an average student, and one of your knuckle-heads. You might as well try to get them all on board from the beginning, eh?

MR. MORRIS

Okay, just these three students are going to demonstrate the procedure when we hear the song. The rest of you should just watch and see how they do.
Looking around at the volunteers:
The song is about thirty seconds long. That should be plenty of time for you to slide your chair under your desk and come to the carpet. You won't need to run or rush.

> If you're a daring, take-a-risk kind of a teacher, you might want to think about playing one of the other songs from the CD. The Andy Griffith theme song, for instance, would be a good one since the whistling is distinctly different from the techno-fusion sounds of Bill Nye. Since you're trying to condition a response to a particular stimulus, playing a different song and watching their reaction might prove to be instructional. (If it were me, I'd probably play the Andy Griffith song just to see how they would handle it. I always like to create situations in which the students are responsible for figuring out the right thing to do. Then again, it might just start a riot. Your call.)

Play the song.[†]

Since the music is going to diminish to effect of your voice anyway, you might as well refrain from offering any comments as you watch your demonstrators demonstrate. Besides, the song is only thirty seconds long. Just wait until it's all over before you jump in.

MR. MORRIS

At the conclusion of the song:
Well, how did they do?

It would be nice if their responses emphasized that the demonstrators were calm and relaxed. They didn't rush. Their chairs are under their desks. When they got to the carpet they just sat quietly. If your students don't come up with these points, which is highly likely, you should try to verbalize them yourself.

MR. MORRIS

To the demonstrators:
Nice job. You may return to your seats.
Turning to the class:
Now we're all going to try it. Remember: calm, relaxed, no rushing, chairs under your desks. And when you do get to the carpet, be ready to pay attention.

---

† If any other students stand up with the chosen demonstrators, just stop the music. Don't say a thing. The interruption of the song should cue them all to sit down. Since you're trying to condition students to respond to a musical cue, you might as well get them used to the fact that you won't be verbally directing every action. Limit the amount of talking you do at this stage in the proceedings. Let the music–or the absence of music–do the talking for you.

Step 11: Everyone Gives It a Try

Play the music and enjoy the performance.

Congratulations. You have successfully introduced a new way to direct your students without having to rely upon your over-used voice. Way to go.

Overview of the Steps You Just Completed

1: Find a CD player that works.

2: Plug it in.

3: Select a song.

4: Become familiar with the song.

5: Assign a procedure to the song.

6: Introduce the song.

7: Play the song.

8: Allow a response.

9: Introduce the procedure.

10: Have students model the procedure.

11: Everyone gives it a try.

Steps to Take in the Future

I think you'll find that your students will do really well the first couple of times you play the song. The novelty of the experience coupled with the clear instructions and demonstration you provided should have everyone conditioned for success. Enjoy it while you can. Before you know it, they'll begin to get a bit lazy and test your resolve. That's okay. It's all part of the learning process.

Step 12: Remind and Review

If it's been a day or two since you used the song, you might want to remind them about the Come to the Carpet procedure before you hit the play button.

The other way to go, which I prefer, is to just play the song and watch their response. I can almost guarantee you'll have a handful of students respond immediately. Without resorting to a verbal intervention, you could allow these students to act as a reminder about what everyone is supposed to do when the *Bill Nye* song is played.

Either way works. It's more a matter of whether you want to reinforce the Old School mindset in which the teacher does all of the instructing and directing and reminding, or if you want to promote and encourage student independence. I know it's easy to remind students about procedures but it doesn't do much for their self-determination.

Step 13: Focus Your Attention

Anticipate that there will be students who begin to test the limits. They will either stay at their desks to finish some task or talk/act out when they get to the carpet. Regardless of the action, whenever you see anything that is outside the bounds of expected behavior, you'll need to intervene. (Don't forget *Setting Limits in the Classroom* by MacKenzie.)

I think the best way to go is to simply write down the names of the offenders and speak to them later on. Don't engage in any kind of verbal redress at the carpet. After all, you wouldn't want to speak to everyone about the actions of a few. Wait until some appropriate time later and deal with it then.

MR. MORRIS
Speaking privately at the beginning of recess:
Calvin, you have a choice. You can do the right thing and come to the carpet when you hear the Bill Nye song or you can see me at recess time. What's your choice?

CALVIN
Slipping into classroom lawyer mode:
But I had to finish my vocabulary assignment.

MR. MORRIS
Not taking the bait:
What are you supposed to do when you hear the music?

CALVIN
Never one to give up easily:
But I had to finish my vocabulary assignment.

MR. MORRIS
Recognizing a denial strategy when he sees one:
We're not talking about that. We're talking about what you're supposed to do when you hear the Bill Nye song.

CALVIN
Finally realizing that the tricks that work with his parents won't work on Mr. Morris:
I'm supposed to get up, put my chair under, and go to the carpet.

MR. MORRIS
With a smile:
That's correct. But when you don't do those three things, then you'll need to see me at recess. What's your choice?

CALVIN
I'll do the three things.

MR. MORRIS
With a pat on Calvin's shoulder:
Good choice. Carry on, please.

Step 14: Sounds vs Songs

Okay, you've now heard *The Science Guy* song more times than you thought possible. Is there another way to achieve the same result? Actually, there is.

After using *Bill Nye* for about two months, I got a bit tired of the piece. I did like the way my students came to the carpet on their own, though, and wanted to keep that part in place. It was just that the music was beginning to wear on me. So I went to Target and bought a five-dollar bicycle bell. You know the kind that straps to the handle bar and has a little thumb lever you push? It makes a distinctive ringing sound and is very easy to use.

Anyway, I attached the bell to the post of my overhead projector which sat on an old TV/VCR stand right next to my desk. (This location made the bell easy to use.) Whenever I wanted my students to join me on the carpet—which happened at least four or five times a day—I just reached over and rang the bell twice. Similar to the stimulus provided by the theme song, the bicycle bell signaled each student to stand up, slide your chair under your desk, and join me on the carpet.

I gained the same benefits as when I used the *Bill Nye* song—a reduction in the use of my voice and an increase in the opportunity for my students to practice self-discipline—while avoiding having to play the song for the 127th time. All in all, everybody won.

Note: The one disadvantage to the use of the bicycle bell was that it lacked the structure created by the song. By playing the *Bill Nye* song, my students knew exactly how long they had to get to the carpet. This helped to keep the pace lively but not tense.

The bell, though, will not establish a time frame. And if you do find yourself having to verbally coerce your students into picking up the pace of the transition, you might want to use the song instead of the sound.

Something to Think About

The classroom is a rich and fluid environment. Although I originally initiated the COME TO THE CARPET procedure with a song, it eventually evolved into just a sound. And that's how it goes. But it only went that way because it was driven there through experience and need.

I guess the point I'm trying to make is that life changes. It starts off in one direction and then veers off into a new one. You can fight it or see where it takes you. That's the beauty of it all; it's your choice. I've learned, though, that it's easier if you're flexible.

So, try new things. Experiment, observe, modify. Just because I say to use music as a cueing technique doesn't mean you need to limit yourself to songs. (*Note:* I did use some songs to signal certain procedures all year long. *Cagney & Lacey*, for instance, alerted my students to the fact that we were about to start our first shared reading activity. *Card Sharks*, played at the end of the day, told everyone we needed to clean up and get ready to depart. Thought you should know.)

So, play around with the whole concept of right-brain signals and see where it takes you and your students.[†] Throughout my career, I was continually surprised at—and encouraged by—how many paths there were that led to a successful environment for learning and growth.

Beyond the Basics

Free Music

You can find a lot of classroom-appropriate music by searching online. Although some of the sites you'll find are just annoyingly difficult to use, there are a couple of them that are well worth your time.

TVTunesOnline.com
This is where I got the songs that are on the CD. It's a user-friendly site that has a ton of great cartoon and television show theme songs. Do yourself a favor and check it out. *BTW:* They used to charge a monthly subscription fee but now it's free.

TelevisionTunes.com
Not as easy to navigate as TVTunesOnline, but still a great source for free music.

FreePlayMusic.com
If you're looking for music to play while your students are working independently, this is the site. The music you'll find meets two critical needs: instrumental and unfamiliar.

---

† Check out Lesson 5 in the *New Management Handbook* for ideas on how to use sound-making toys to communicate with your students.

Songs without lyrics will make it easier for your students to concentrate on the task at hand. This will be most significant during the first couple of weeks of music use. After a bit of experience, though, they will be able to listen to just about any kind of music yet still stay on task.

And by playing music your students don't recognize, you won't have to worry about any preconceived notions and opinions about the music. It'll be a clean slate.

Classroom Sign Language

Back on page 69, I talked about using a couple of signs to send messages to my students during my introduction of the *Bill Nye* song. Similar to the power of using a song to initiate a procedure, the use of sign language was another great way to communicate without having to use my over-used voice. I started off each year with just five simple signs. By the end of the year we were using 40 or 50 of them.[†]

Anyway, here are the two signs I used.

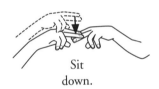

Sit
down.

That was off-topic.

power
love
fun
freedom
safety

The footnote at the bottom of page 69 dealt with a situation in which a student—or three—mistakenly stood up when I verbalized that step in the *Bill Nye* procedure. By using the "sit down" sign, I wouldn't have had to use my voice in a negative way.

A little farther up the page—in Step 8, to be exact—I recommended that you allow your students to share their thoughts regarding the *Bill Nye* song you had just played for them. This doesn't mean, though, that it's suddenly open season for them to share any random thoughts that happen to pop into their heads. Granted, some of their comments will be appropriate; nonetheless, others won't.

To deal with the inappropriate comments, I just showed the student the "that was off-topic" sign. While the sign lingered in the air for a moment, I looked for someone else to add to our wonderfully stimulating ode to Mr. Bill Nye, the Science Guy.

Without this simple sign, I may have fallen into the Old School habit of verbally sharing my displeasure at the not-what-we-were-looking-for comment.

[†]   Check out the book, *Tools & Toys*, for a lesson on how to begin using sign language with your students..

MR. MORRIS

Sounding a bit like Blackbeard:

WE'RE NOT TALKING ABOUT YOUR BROTHER'S GARAGE BAND!
WE'RE TALKING ABOUT THE BILL NYE SONG!

The non-emotional sign language beat the negative verbal message by a wide margin.†

Bonus: If you would like a set of mini-posters to display in your classroom as a reference for you and your students, you can download them from the New Management website. There are 14 posters that show 15 different signs.

Double Bonus: There's a very cool website that will show you, with videos, how to sign specific words. The URL is http://commtechlab.msu.edu/sites/aslweb/browser.htm

TV Theme Song Playlists

To make it easier to find the song you want to play, you might want to reproduce the blackline master found on the next page. The three playlists can be placed in your room in different spots as a quick reference guide. Although the songs are printed on the CD, it's going to be hard to read the titles when the CD is inside the player.

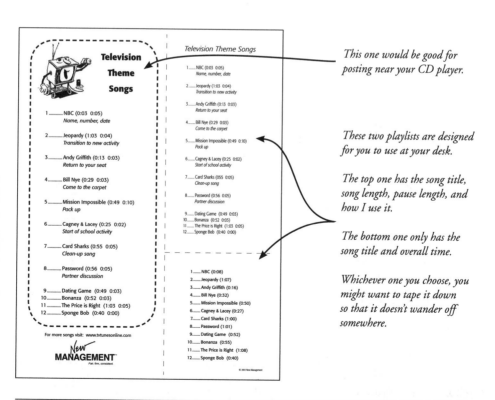

FIG. 4-1
There are two times shown for each song.

The first one is the actual playing time.

The second one shows the length of the pause before the next song begins.

---

† The research done on the disparity between the amount of positive comments being made versus the amount of negative comments being made paints a rather sad picture. In the average classroom, there is a positive comment every four minutes. There's a negative one every 20 seconds. Ouch.

Television

Theme

Songs

1 .... NBC (0:03 0:05)
Name, number, date

2 .... Jeopardy (1:03 0:04)
Transition to new activity

3 .... Andy Griffith (0:13 0:03)
Return to your seat

4 .... Bill Nye (0:29 0:03)
Come to the carpet

5 .... Mission Impossible (0:49 0:10)
Pack up

6 .... Cagney & Lacey (0:25 0:02)
Start of school activity

7 .... Card Sharks (0:55 0:05)
Clean-up song

8 .... Password (0:56 0:05)
Partner discussion

9 .... Dating Game (0:49 0:03)
10 .... Bonanza (0:52 0:03)
11 .... The Price is Right (1:03 0:05)
12 .... Sponge Bob (0:40 0:00)

For more songs visit: www.tvtunesonline.com

New
MANAGEMENT™
Fair, firm, consistent.

Television Theme Songs

1 .... NBC (0:03 0:05)
Name, number, date

2 .... Jeopardy (1:03 0:04)
Transition to new activity

3 .... Andy Griffith (0:13 0:03)
Return to your seat

4 .... Bill Nye (0:29 0:03)
Come to the carpet

5 .... Mission Impossible (0:49 0:10)
Pack up

6 .... Cagney & Lacey (0:25 0:02)
Start of school activity

7 .... Card Sharks (055 0:05)
Clean-up song

8 .... Password (0:56 0:05)
Partner discussion

9 .... Dating Game (0:49 0:03)
10 .... Bonanza (0:52 0:03)
11 .... The Price is Right (1:03 0:05)
12 .... Sponge Bob (0:40 0:00)

---

1 .... NBC (0:08)
2 .... Jeopardy (1:07)
3 .... Andy Griffith (0:16)
4 .... Bill Nye (0:32)
5 .... Mission Impossible (0:50)
6 .... Cagney & Lacey (0:27)
7 .... Card Sharks (1:00)
8 .... Password (1:01)
9 .... Dating Game (0:52)
10 .... Bonanza (0:55)
11 .... The Price is Right (1:08)
12 .... Sponge Bob (0:40)

Chapter Five

Core Principles

Confessions of a Former Echoer

The Top Ten Things I Said

Using Music for
Student Independence

Sentence Strips
Cut-and-Paste Paragraphs

Homework Made Easier

Behavior CODES

Credit Cards

*The desire to write
grows with writing.*

— Erasmus

Chapter 5
Sentence Strips
Cut-and-Paste Paragraphs

◆ ◆

Goals for this chapter:

☑ Realize that you sometimes need to be flexible to meet the needs of your students.

☑ Discover how Sentence Strips can make paragraph writing manageable.

☑ Develop a new writing, editing, and correcting procedure to use with your students.

☑ Learn a new set of simple, yet effective, proofreading marks.

◆ ◆

So, anyway, there we were, working away on our paragraphs about last Friday's whale watching field trip. Our ultimate goal was to produce a class book about our adventure at sea. Having already engaged in various pre-writing activities, e.g., verbalizing, retelling favorite parts of the trip, sharing sketches we had done the day before, creating a word bank, etc., the students were at that moment desperately groping their way through The Land of the Rough Draft.[†]

Twenty minutes into it and the first rough draftee appeared on the horizon. It was Calvin. He placed his paragraph on my desk with something less than a flourish of pride.

A quick scan of his woefully malnourished collection of sentences had me reaching for my red correcting pen and a couple of Tylenol.

power
love
fun
freedom
safety

MR. MORRIS
Trying to make the best of it:
Okay, Calvin. Not bad for a start. How about if you check the spelling of these words [circle, circle, circle, circle, long circle, circle, circle]; check for punctuation here [check mark], here [check mark] and here [check mark]; move this sentence

---

†   I actually stopped calling their first attempts at writing a "rough draft" and used "first draft" instead. This term implied that there might be more than one revision during the writing process.

up here [long curving arrow]; get rid of this sentence [slash] and this sentence [slash]; make these letters capital letters [underline, underline, underline] and, uh, rewrite it as neatly as you can.

And then, with my best large and encouraging smile, I handed back his paragraph which now looked as if it had undergone open heart surgery. Unsuccessful open heart surgery.

CALVIN
    Not terribly thrilled by the prospect:
        Write it over?
    Long face, slumping shoulders:
        I thought I was done.

MR. MORRIS
    Ever the encourager:
        You don't want your paragraph to look like this, do you? You've got some good ideas here. They just need a bit of work. Rewrite it, and you will be done. Okay?

Well, apparently it wasn't okay. Calvin, academic dilettante that he was, dragged his sad self back to his seat, slammed his paragraph down on his desk, and proceeded to cry.

Cry? This kid's crying about his whale watching paragraph? Hey, if anyone should have been crying over that piece of work, it should have been me. Nonetheless, there he was, wailing and gnashing his teeth because Mr. Morris was asking him to do a quality job. What was a dedicated professional to do?

I suppose I could have done what I had sometimes done in the past—self-righteously laid Calvin's frustration and failure at his feet.

After all, hadn't I made a serious effort to get him started in the right direction?

I sure had.

And wasn't I merely looking out for Calvin's best interests by maintaining high, albeit attainable, expectations of language achievement?

I sure was.

If he was going to just wimp out after all of my well-intentioned effort and good will, well, too bad. He was going to have to deal with his rather anemic writing skills sometime in his life. What better sometime than third grade? Come on, Calvin, be a man. Rewrite that paragraph.

But this was where I chose to zag instead of zig. As opposed to following the conventional path of "it's his problem, not mine," I decided to figure out a way to help him overcome his difficulties. After all, maybe there was some validity to Calvin's point of view. Maybe this time-honored method of creative writing just wasn't going to meet his needs no matter how hard he tried. And just what, exactly, had brought Calvin to his literary knees? I didn't know at the moment, but I sure wanted to find out. Why not put off the writing for a day until I could give it some deep thought?

MR. MORRIS
  Addressing the entire class:
    Tell you what, guys. Why don't we put
    away our paragraphs for right now.
    We'll work on them again tomorrow.

At the end of the day I went home, put on my skates, plugged in my headphones, and headed for the boardwalk. I found this to be one of my favorite problem-solving modes. The music and movement seemed to get me in a right-brained zone, and experience had shown that using both halves of my brain oft times produced some real breakthrough thinking.

And just what, exactly, had brought Calvin to his literary knees? I didn't know at the moment, but I sure wanted to find out.

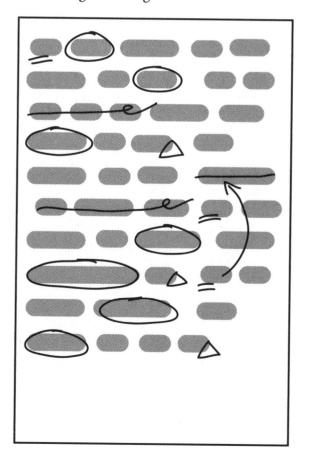

FIG. 5-1
Calvin's global view of his paragraph was causing understandable feelings of frustration and failure.

As I skated along, I focused on Calvin, his frustration, and his 98-pound weakling of a paragraph. I got to looking at the underlying structure of what he had been facing. I could picture Calvin sitting at his desk staring miserably at his slashed and burned bit of writing, not to mention his feelings twenty minutes prior as he stared miserably at his blank piece of paper.

I could almost feel his sense of being overwhelmed by the prospect of having to rewrite so much of what he had already written. It was just too much for a poorly skilled little third grader to face.

If only I could have gotten my hands on his thoughts before he committed them to paper. If only I could help him to realize how fundamentally simple a paragraph can be when

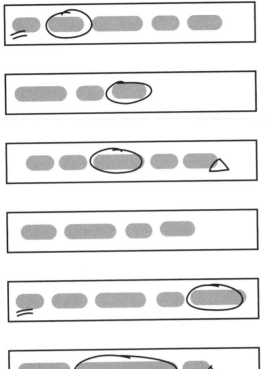

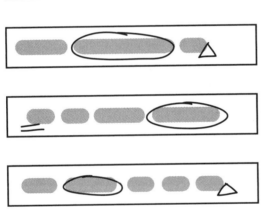

Fig. 5-2
A more manageable view of his same paragraph as separate blocks of sentences allowed for a sentence-by-sentence focus and a growing sense of confidence and accomplishment.

thoughts are successfully written one at a time.

And that's when, as they say, it hit me.

My right brain, in its wonderfully non-verbal way, enabled me see that a writing road block had been created by the mere format of Calvin's paragraph. Having all eight sentences crammed together on one piece of paper had trapped him into a global view of his work. And the global view was not pretty. There were oceans of red: red circles, slashes, arrows, check marks, and underlines with very few land masses of coherent meaning and grammatical convention.

What was needed, I realized, was a simple technique which would reinforce the one-sentence-at-a-time-awareness so that his sense of being overwhelmed by the demands of the entire piece would become reduced and thus manageable. This new procedure would also have to be manageable for me since Calvin wasn't the only "Calvin" I was working with that year.

How about using different paper?

We could replace the standard sheet of paper with narrow strips large enough for just one sentence. And then, instead of writing his entire paragraph in one shot, he'd write just one sentence at a time. He could check it over and maybe share it with a neighbor. Then, after I had had a chance to review it, he could make revisions as necessary, and then move on to the next sentence.

Having the sentences on separate pieces of paper would also allow him to play around with the sequencing or even make room for additional sentences. The possibilities for building success and confidence as an author seemed truly enormous. And if not, it at least seemed to be worth a try.

Suitably armed with the glimmerings of a new approach to the fundamental writing process, I returned to class the next day with an equally new attitude.

To keep myself from overwhelming the students with both my own excitement and this novel technique, I decided to present the "Sentence Strip" concept over the next five days, forty minutes per day.

Day One: An Idea List

Using their previously written thoughts about the whale watching trip as a starting point, I asked them to compile a list of ideas they would like to include in their paragraph.

> The emphasis here was on *ideas*, not sentences. I wanted notes—just a word or two—which would encapsulate the idea. Writing just one word would also prevent anyone from getting bogged down in unnecessary detail.

MR. MORRIS
In a calm, relaxed manner:
Just make a simple list of what you want to include in your paragraph. Don't worry about what order it's in. Don't worry about spelling. Just let your thoughts flow. In fact, close your eyes for just a moment.
Pausing for students to realize he's serious about closing their eyes:
Now, visualize our whale watching trip.
Another pause:
Just make a list of what you are seeing.

To help get them started, we took a few suggestions for ideas and made a simple story map on the whiteboard.

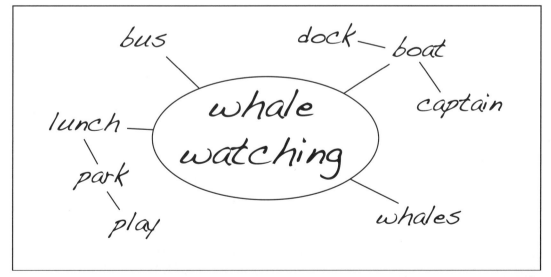

FIG. 5-3
This type of story map—a graphical organizer, if you will—really helps the visual learners to be more successful.

Each idea was accompanied by an explanation about what the word meant. For example, the idea behind "lunch" was that someone wanted to write about the fact we had eaten lunch at the park after the whale watching trip.

After ten minutes of independent idea generation, we stopped for an Author Talk.[†]

Several volunteers read their idea lists. Some were 4-5 ideas in length, others were in the 9-10 range. No limit or minimum had been set.

MR. MORRIS
Anticipating the question:
If you were to ask how many ideas you need to have, I'd say that it's up to you. Whatever it takes to tell your story should be your guide.

During this Author Talk, students were allowed—encouraged, actually—to add to their Idea Lists if they heard an idea they wanted to include. Also, due to the synergy of idea sharing, students added new ideas which came to them as they listened to other Idea Lists. This brief period of active listening helped to reinforce the philosophy that there is more to writing than putting a pencil to a piece of paper. After the Author Talk, everyone was allowed to work on his Idea List for the remainder of our forty-minute writing period.

Day Two: Sentence Strips

The first order of business was to prepare a supply of what would soon be referred to as Sentence Strips. I took some 8 1/2 x 11 lined newsprint and chopped it on the paper cutter like this:

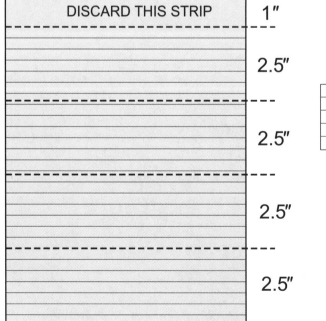

FIG. 5-4
I like newsprint because it's cheap and there's tons of it in our supply room.

I save the pretty stuff (white foolscap) for the final draft.

DISCARD THIS STRIP   1"

2.5"

2.5"

2.5"

2.5"

Calvin #6

Note: Writing paper with printed margin lines might be better than plain newsprint since it provides a ready-made space for a student to write his name and number.

---

† This was our phrase for when students orally shared their writing with the class. Nothing fancy. I just thought we should all be on the same page in regard to the language we used in my classroom.

The second order of business was to prepare an editing sheet. This simple chart would explain the proofreading marks we would be using for this writing activity.

The chart looked like this:

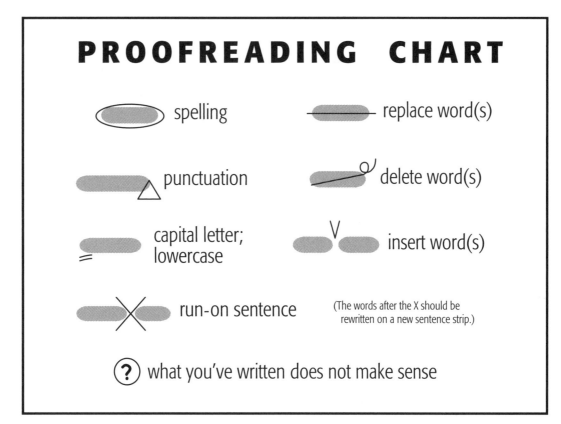

FIG. 5-5
This proof-reading chart can be found on the last page of this chapter.

On the same page you'll find a flow-chart your students can use as a guide for the Sentence Strips writing process.

It was then time to introduce the basic Sentence Strip process.

MR. MORRIS
With everything he needed within reach:
Today you will be turning your ideas into sentences. For each idea on your Idea List you'll write one sentence. These sentences will be written on small pieces of paper.
Holding up a Sentence Strip:
This is called a Sentence Strip and can be found in this box.
Holding up the box that contains the 400-500 pre-cut Sentence Strips:
Take a look at your first idea. Think about what you wanted to say about that idea. After you've thought for a bit, write your thought on a Sentence Strip. Share this sentence with a friend or two and then bring it to me for checking. If it's okay the way it's written, I'll put a plus on it, and you will have successfully written your first sentence. If it needs some revision, you'll get another Sentence Strip and redo your sentence.

After a bit of Q & A, we were ready to begin. I set our class timer for twenty minutes, and the students began writing.

It was, from the beginning, an unqualified success.

Freed from the overwhelming stress of having to produce a complete paragraph, the students were able to devote their energies to writing individual sentences. This one simple step made the entire writing process manageable for everyone in our class. Writing one sentence was something just about everyone could do with some degree of success.

Within a few minutes I had my first sentence to check.

Mr. Morris
    Placing Calvin's sentence on his desk:
        Well, let's see what you have here.

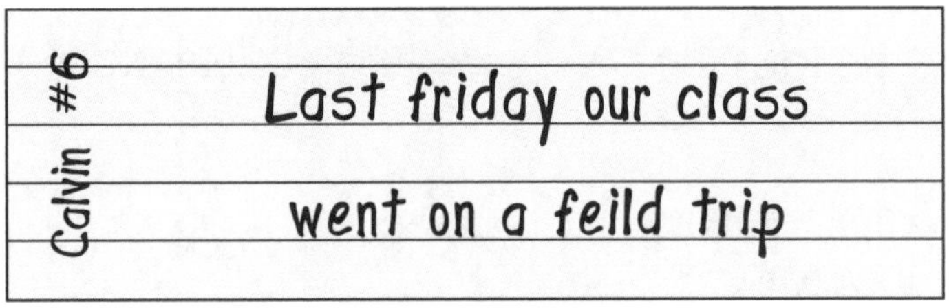

Fig. 5-6
Here we see Calvin's sentence the way he had written it.

> #6
> Calvin
> Last friday our class
> went on a feild trip

    Marking two lines under the f in friday:
        Let's capitalize the word "Friday."

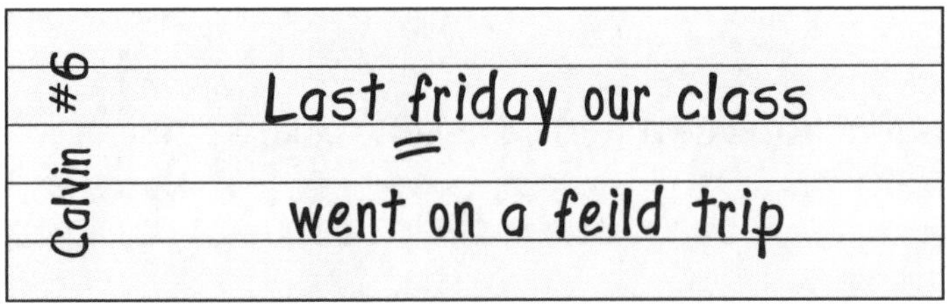

Fig. 5-7
The two little lines under the letter "f" indicate a capitalization mistake.

> #6
> Calvin
> Last friday our class
> =
> went on a feild trip

    Circling feild:
        Check the spelling of the word "field."

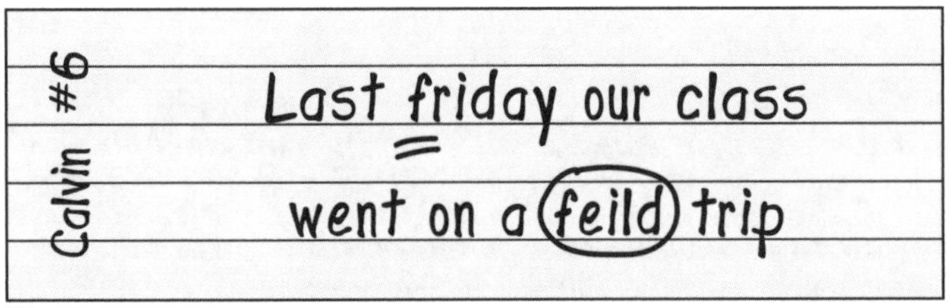

Fig. 5-8
I circled the word "feild" because it was not spelled correctly.

> #6
> Calvin
> Last friday our class
> =
> went on a (feild) trip

    Drawing a triangle at the end of the sentence:
        And think about some kind of sentence-ending punctuation.

Fig. 5-9
The triangle is used for any and all punctuation mistakes.

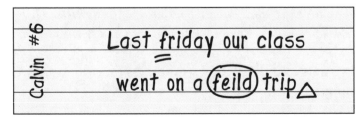

MR. MORRIS
power
love
fun
freedom
safety

    Handing back the now-edited sentence with a smile:
       You're off to a good start. Rewrite this on another strip, and I'll put a plus on it for you.
       By the way, did you happen to share this sentence with a friend?

Sheepish look.

MR. MORRIS
power
love
fun
freedom
safety

    Remaining calm because new procedures take time and practice:
       Please make sure you share your sentence with another student before coming to see me.
       Thanks.

Elapsed time: 11 seconds.

Ah, here comes another one.

FIG. 5-10
Anna's sentence is shown in its original form. Other than it being rather drab, it was mistake-free.

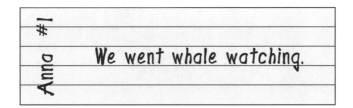

In this type of situation, there were two ways I could go.

First of all, I could mark it with a plus and return it with a smile and a plus. Since it started with a capital letter, ended with the proper punctuation, contained no spelling mistakes, and made sense, this sentence was acceptable as written. And for the poorly skilled writer, that's probably what I would do. Approving this first attempt would build confidence and encourage him to tackle his next idea. As much as I might have wanted to develop this sentence into something more expressive or comprehensive, it was equally important to maintain realistic expectations.

power
love
fun
freedom
safety

The other approach, which could be used to stimulate and develop the writing skills of the more confident writer, would be to suggest some changes.

MR. MORRIS
    Underlining the word "we" and asking:
       Who went whale watching?

FIG. 5-11
To stimulate the writing process, I underscored a word that could be expanded into something more detailed.

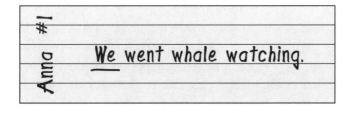

Mr. Morris
Planting a couple of carets after the word "watching" and suggesting:
You know, you might want to add some kind of a time or place reference here.

Fig. 5-12
Carets are used for a missing word or two. They're also designed to encourage students to add clarity.

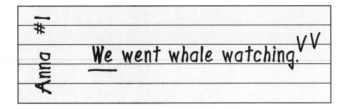

And now, having received her prompts, Anna would pick up another Sentence Strip and rewrite the same sentence so that it included the necessary details. When completed, it would again be shared and then rechecked. After approval, this sentence would become the first in a growing collection of edited sentences.

The Line

It wasn't long before I had a line of students waiting to have their sentences checked. This meant there had been lots of writing and reviewing effort. It also meant that they were going to have to wait awhile before they got to see me. Was this line going to create a problem or was there an opportunity lurking?

As it turned out, the line of waiting students became an additional step in the writing process. Instead of trying to impose some type of artificial calm and quiet on this waiting queue, we turned it into a forum. We decided upon a simple procedure.

When you get in line:
1. Switch sentences with the person in front of you.
2. Read the sentence and check it for corrections or suggestions.
3. Give it back and share your thoughts.
4. Switch with someone else and repeat the process.

Some students ended up leaving the line when simple errors were pointed out to them. After all, I certainly wasn't the only one who could see that Calvin's sentence needed some kind of punctuation at the end. More importantly, though, many students were able to take back a detail, a phrase, or an idea to add to their own paragraphs. The line provided the kind of dynamic interaction that really stimulates young, or inexperienced, writers.

Twenty minutes later, when the timer went off, we stopped for an Author Talk. This time, several students were able to share their approved sentences. After a pause for student commentary and a review of the three-step writing procedure—write, share, get it checked—we attempted another twenty minute writing period. At the end of this second period, they put their materials in their envelopes. (See page 98 for an example of this.)

Day Three: Sentence Strips II

The third day found us heavily involved in the basic Sentence Strip process. What a refreshing change. Instead of having students staring at a half filled sheet of paper, I was seeing them eagerly grabbing new Sentence Strips to pen their next thoughts. So many of them got caught up in the writing process that they cured themselves of the how-many-sentences-do-I-have-to-write syndrome.

And now, on the third day of writing using this new technique, we began to experience one of the truly powerful aspects of Sentence Strips: the freedom to manipulate a paragraph without having to rewrite the whole thing.

It went like this:

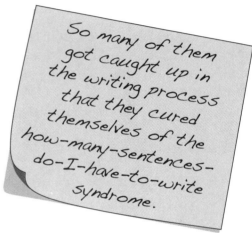

So many of them got caught up in the writing process that they cured themselves of the how-many-sentences-do-I-have-to-write syndrome.

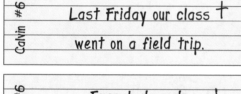

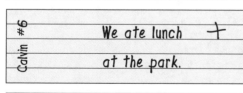

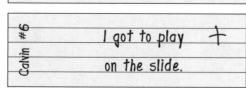

FIG. 5-13
Calvin's collection of sentences that he has brought to my desk and laid out in the proper order.

As an option, you could have Calvin lay out his sentences on his own desk. When he's ready, he could then come get you to check his writing.

CALVIN
Obviously proud but also a bit nervous:
I'm done, Mr. Morris.

MR. MORRIS
Calm and relaxed:
Well, let's see what you've written.

Calvin laid his six edited Sentence Strips on my desk. (Fig. 5-13)

MR. MORRIS
With a sincere display of appreciation:
This is great, Calvin. You've got some really good ideas here.

Big smile from Calvin. His worst fears of rejection or failure had evaporated. In its place, his new-found success left him feeling energized to engage in a brief discussion on how to become a better writer.

MR. MORRIS
Gently:
Would you mind if I offer a couple of suggestions?

CALVIN
   Not sure what's coming and, as a result, a bit leery:
   Uh, okay.

MR. MORRIS
   How about if we save your feelings about the trip for the end of your paragraph?

I reached out and moved sentence #4 to the bottom of the group of sentences. Painless.

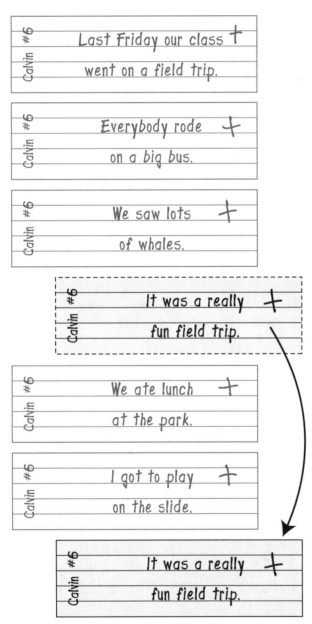

FIG. 5-14
It is so easy
for students
to rearrange
their written
thoughts
when each
one is on its
own piece
of paper.

CALVIN
   Somewhat stunned by how simple it was to make the change:
   Oh, yeah! I like that better.

MR. MORRIS

Offering another simple idea:

And you know, you kind of jump from 'seeing whales' to 'eating lunch at the park.'
Maybe you could write one more sentence about what happened after we saw whales or
how we got to the park.

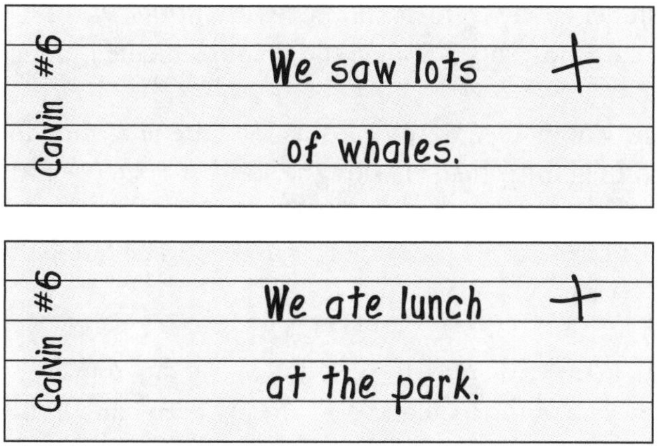

FIG. 5-15
These two
sentences
ended up
together
after we
had moved
the fourth
sentence to
the bottom
of the list.

Zoom! He was off.

The success and confidence he had gained from writing his other six sentences encouraged him to expand his paragraph while the flexibility of the Sentence Strip procedure made the revision remarkably simple.

Just move this sentence out of the way, add one sentence here, and Bingo! You've got your-self a new and improved paragraph.

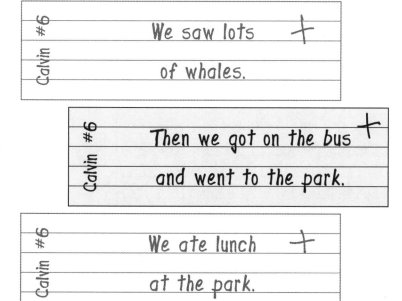

FIG. 5-16
It's a
manageable
thing for
a student
to grab
one more
piece of
paper, pen
one more
sentence,
and add to
the overall
quality of
the whole
paragraph.

Day Four: First Draft

We started with an Author Talk. This provided an opportunity to share our thoughts and opinions about what had been written during the past two days.

As paragraphs were read, students offered their comments about the writing. And with the flexibility of the Sentence Strips, suggestions could be implemented immediately.

After hearing from everyone who wished to read, I explained the procedure for writing a first draft. This step was nothing more than checking to see that Sentence Strips were in the proper order and then copying them one at a time onto a letter-sized sheet of lined newsprint. The only stipulations were: 1) the sentences needed to be numbered, and 2) a space was to be left between each sentence.

Seeing all of their sentences in order on one sheet would enable me to make a final review of each paragraph. And, since all of the sentences had already been edited, this final review was a much simpler task than I normally would have faced. Spelling, punctuation, and missing words were at a minimum; therefore, I was able to focus on content and continuity. Duplicate thoughts could get deleted, and order could be established by renumbering the out-of-order sentences.

Calvin #6   First Draft

1. Last Friday my class went whale watching.

2. Everybody rode on a big bus.

3. We saw lots of whales.

4. Then we got on the bus and went to the park.

5. We ate lunch at the park.

6. I got to play on the slide.

7. It was a really fun field trip.

FIG. 5-17
By having the students skips spaces between the sentences, I had room to make corrections or offer suggestions.

A woman wrote to me about her experience using Sentence Strips and shared this clever tip:

"I have my students glue their sentences onto a sheet of butcher paper with glue sticks. They like this because it feels like an art project. Or maybe they just like not having to copy all of their sentences onto a new sheet of paper. Either way, it's something they look forward to and is also a nice change of pace after all of the writing and revision."

Day Five: The Final Draft

After introducing the basic paragraph format, the first drafts were passed back and discussed. A supply of white lined paper was made available. I popped in a CD of some soothing music and set the timer.

To help reinforce how a paragraph was supposed to be formatted, I asked everyone to bring me their final draft after they had written their name, date, title, and the first word of the first sentence. I wanted to establish where the second line should begin since it was a combination of the first word and the second line which created the indentation. After seeing them for this initial contact, they were then free to complete their final drafts.

At the end of that week, I was able to harvest thirty-one well-written paragraphs which we later compiled into a class book. And the students, for their part, had learned a simple writing process that would help them become more proficient writers. After all, writing a paragraph about a field trip wasn't going to be very helpful in life; however, knowing how to write a paragraph would prove to be quite useful indeed.

Former Students Speak Out

I liked Sentence Strips because I wrote one sentence at a time. Writing one sentence at a time made it easier to check them over. Sentence Strips also kept my thoughts from getting all jammed together.

—Angel Ramon, third grade student

Sentence Strips helped me become a better writer. Using this idea allowed me to focus on one sentence instead of many. Then I was able to rearrange them so that the sentences fit together correctly.

—Amanda Abeln, fifth grade student

The Sentence Strip method worked very well for me. It helped me write clear, descriptive sentences. It also gave me a chance to switch the sentences around without having to erase them or rewrite my whole paragraph.

—Dang Nguyen, sixth grade student

Sentence Strips helped me on my journey of writing intelligent essays and reports. In our class, we would write individual sentences on strips of paper and then take them to our teacher or classmates for their opinions. That led me to writing and proofreading on a higher level. I not only learned to find grammatical errors, but also to look into the meaning of what I'd written to analyze it or make changes.

—Robyn Barbrick, former student now in high school

Beyond the Basics

I used the basic Sentence Strip technique for more than twenty years and, like most of the things we do in the classroom, it got better with age. Some of this improvement was due to the experience I gained with use: the "practice makes better" school of thinking. The additional improvement—a *kaizen* thing, previously defined on page 66—came about through modification and adaptation.

Here, then, are a few thoughts I'd like to add to the original Sentence Strip article which was first published in the *Writing Notebook* back in 1992.

Everyone writing the same thing

Although it was not absolutely necessary, I discovered that Sentence Strips worked really well when everyone was working on the same topic. This will be especially true for your initial attempts at using this technique.

The advantage for me was that I knew what each student was writing about even before the sentence was placed on my desk. It made the editing process a bit quicker and more focused.

The advantage for the students had to do with the advice they were able to receive from their classmates. As you read earlier in this chapter, everyone was writing about the whale watching field trip and so they all had a common topic. When a student switched sentences with another student for checking, the help they offered each other was more effective since there was extensive background knowledge of vocabulary and subject matter in play. Also, students waiting in line to see me were able to read ideas from other students that they could later incorporate into their own paragraphs.

This doesn't mean that you should limit Sentence Strips to situations in which your students are all working on the same assignment. It's just that you might want to use this technique in those situations until your class is comfortable with it.

Just one sentence

An issue I can almost guarantee you're going to face is this: a student will bring you more than one sentence to correct. I'm not sure why this happens, but it does. Whenever this happened, I just corrected the one sentence and handed back the others. This meant, of course, that the student had to get back in line. That was okay. Leaving my desk with only one of the sentences edited reinforced my request to only bring one sentence at a time. *Reality:* If you verbally remind a student but check all of the sentences anyway, you'll just end up seeing more students with more than one sentence. And editing multiple sentences for multiple students, I learned, really bogged down the line.

Two sentences

Although the original idea was to have a student bring a sentence for editing and then return with the corrected sentence, you may not want to go that way after your students have mastered the Sentence Strips procedure. It's actually more efficient if the child brings back the corrected sentence when he is coming to see you with his new one. This will eliminate a student's need to wait in line to show you that, yes, there is now a capital letter at the beginning of the sentence.

If you try this simple adaptation, you'll need to decide upon a correction procedure.

1. Rewrite the entire sentence

Although it may seem unnecessary to rewrite an entire sentence because of, say, one little capitalization error, it may actually cause them to work more carefully on future sentences. On the other hand, their dread of having to rewrite the whole sentence might cause them to be less bold in their writing.

For example, think about the student who would use a word he already knew how to spell in lieu of a higher-level word that is difficult to spell. You certainly wouldn't want any students to take fewer risks as authors due to their understandable concern about having to rewrite an entire sentence.

Additionally, the rewritten sentence sometimes caused a bit of initial confusion when a student would present two sentences. Which was the corrected one and which was the new one to be edited? Although he knew that he was supposed to show me the corrected sentence first, it didn't always happen. This meant that I didn't always know which of the two sentences I had already seen. A small issue, granted, but an issue nonetheless.

2. Just fix the mistake

The other way to go, which is the method I preferred, was to have them just fix the mistakes. If, as mentioned above, I had drawn two little lines under the first letter of the first word to indicate a lower case/upper case problem, the child could just erase the letter and rewrite it properly. When he returned to see me with his new sentence, I would have been able to easily identify the one he had corrected. It would be the one with my editing marks. I would give it a quick scan to verify that it was correct, a quicker plus sign to show that it was now correct as is, and then I could have turned my full attention to the new sentence.

The envelope, please

Over the years, we tried various methods for keeping the Sentence Strips and Idea Lists organized. To save you the same grief, here's the hands-down winner: ordinary envelopes. An envelope will not only hold everything a student needs until the project has been completed, but will also reduce desk clutter.

As you can see below, Calvin has written his name and number in the return address area and the title of the writing project in the place normally used for the mailing address. It's the simple ideas that help us to maintain our collective sanity.

FIG. 5-18
A letter-sized envelope will hold the Idea List, the finished sentence strips, and a small supply of blank strips for new sentences.

> Calvin Hobbes #6
>
> Whale Watching
> Field Trip

Using a simple letter-sized envelope is so easy to do that Calvin will actually use it. If classroom management techniques are too difficult, students won't use them.

Student editors

power
love
fun
freedom
safety

If you have several gifted writers in your room, you might want to put them to work. Since they're not going to need a great deal of your serious intervention with their own writing, you should take advantage of their skills and allow them to help out as assistant editors.

The easiest method is to set them up at their own table. Announce to the class that prior to anyone bringing a sentence directly to you, the sentence needs to go to one of the assistants. This will free you from tedious repetitions of "You need to begin your sentence with a capital," while providing you with more time to help with the serious work of guiding students to develop their writing skills, and so become authors.

Important factor: The assistants will still be working on their own sentences. They'll just do it when there isn't someone in front of them needing attention.

Hatchet book report

There are, as you can now imagine, a variety of ways in which you could use Sentence Strips to energize your writing program while making assignments more manageable for your less-than-skilled students.

We used it one year as a way to write book reports based upon the novel I was reading to them. It was a fifth grade class, and I was reading Gary Paulsen's terrific book, *Hatchet*. Each day, at two different times, I would read enough of the book to cover something significant. At the end of each reading, I would have them write a sentence that summed up what had just occurred. After spending a few minutes writing, we would have students share what they thought was the main idea. (During these Author Talks, students were always welcome to change or edit what they'd written based upon what they had just heard.) Six weeks later, when we had finished the book, everyone had an envelope that was stuffed full of sentences.

To write their book reports, the students placed their sentences on their desks and then arranged them into groups. There were sentences about food, sentences about the shelter the boy had built, sentences about the animals he had encountered, etc. They then wrote main idea sentences for these "paragraph" groups, put the paragraphs into some kind of logical order, and ended up with some really beautiful reports.

At the end of the project, the class was delighted with not only the quality of their final reports but also the ease with which they had been written.

A class letter

Why not try this idea with the whole class helping to write a friendly letter of thanks to someone? You could cut up large strips of newsprint (12" x 36") for your strips. As the students offered ideas or suggestions for the letter, they could be given one of the strips and a felt-tip marker to write it out. These sentences could then be taped to the board for everyone to see. You would have the same Sentence Strip flexibility to change or modify the letter without having to redo any of the writing.

Numbering sentences

Although some students will number their Sentence Strips as they write them, my recommendation is to hold off on numbering until the first draft. Students sometimes get trapped into thinking that the first sentence they wrote has to stay #1 even though they may end up writing another sentence that would be a better lead.

By not numbering the sentences, your students will be more inclined to move one of their sentences to a different spot. Also, the daily practice of sentence sequencing as they lay out their collection of sentences for the new writing session is, I think, beneficial.

Beyond Sentence Strips

About halfway through the year, after we had used the basic Sentence Strip technique for many, many writing activities, I added a slight variation. Instead of using one strip of paper for each sentence, they wrote all of them on one large sheet of paper. They still wrote them in the basic one-at-a-time fashion and had each one checked, but all of the sentences were written on one sheet with a space between each one.

There are several advantages to this method. For one, it was easier for me to check on continuity of thought since I was able to see all of the sentences at one time. This was especially helpful when everyone was writing about a different topic.

Another benefit was that it was much easier for the students to hang on to the entire piece of writing. The sentence-strips-in-the-envelope method worked great; nonetheless, having just one piece of paper to keep track of was about as simple as it got.

Lastly, writing all of the sentences on one sheet more closely modeled the actual writing experience most of them would be using as they continued through school. After all, Sentence Strips was just a bridge to better writing. It wasn't a destination itself.

There are a couple of issues to address, though, before you try this variation.

Fixing mistakes
As I mentioned on page 97, there are two ways to go.

The easy way for you is to have the student rewrite the entire sentence in the space below the original sentence. The corrections can then be checked when the student is bringing you his new sentence.

I still preferred to have them just fix the mistakes. It made things a bit messier, I know, but that was okay. (They're kids; they like things messy.) When he returned to see me with his new sentence, I would then be able to check the revision of the previous one.

Inserting new sentences
The bigger issue to the one-sheet-of-paper process—which was what inspired the Sentence Strips strategy in the first place—was the inability to easily rearrange sentences. To alleviate this shortcoming, we came up with an insertion procedure.

Whenever a student wanted to add a sentence between two sentences that were already written, he would write a number in the margin between the two lines of writing. (*Remember:* We didn't number sentences as we wrote them.) The number was circled to help it stand out. The student then wrote the same number next to an empty space on the paper and wrote the sentence to insert. Later on, during the production of the first draft, he'd know to insert the added sentence when he came to the circled number.

Using the Blackline Master

The blackline master on page 102—there's no page number but you'll figure it out—is for you to reproduce and share with your students. It's composed of the editing marks we used and a writing-process flowchart.

Editing marks

The editing marks were the ones we used for all of our written writing. Although our most recently adopted language arts handbook presented the students with about 20 different marks, I didn't think we needed them all. Instead of using a mark to indicate, "Place a quotation mark here," I just used our little triangle. The triangle meant "punctuation" anyway, and the problem-solving that the students went through as they figured out what *type* of punctuation was needed was, in my opinion, good for them.

Suggestion: One teacher told me she makes the editing marks in the margins. The students must then find the mistake in that line of writing. Very nice.

Flowchart

The flowchart was designed to make the initial Sentence Strips experience a bit more successful for everyone. It was a simple road map that helped me to avoid having to remind my students, over and over again, about the proper journey each sentence must undertake in order for it to be approved for use in the finished product.

Before too long, "Check the chart" will become an automatic part of your vocabulary. *Better:* Write the words on a name tag and wear it. You won't need to say a thing.

Stick With It

Last suggestion.

I was talking with a teaching friend of mine one day by the name of Mark Epley. He's been teaching for many years and has been using Sentence Strips ever since he was a student teacher. The one thing he wanted me to pass along to teachers trying this technique was this:

> *"Give it some time. It takes a number of Sentence Strips sessions*
> *in order for you and your students to gain an understanding*
> *of how the whole thing works. It's going to be a bit rocky*
> *the first couple of times you try this idea. That's normal*
> *for any new experience. Just work through it, learn from it,*
> *and visualize how great it's going to be when everyone*
> *has it down and is writing like a pro."*

Thanks, Mark. Well said.

PROOFREADING CHART

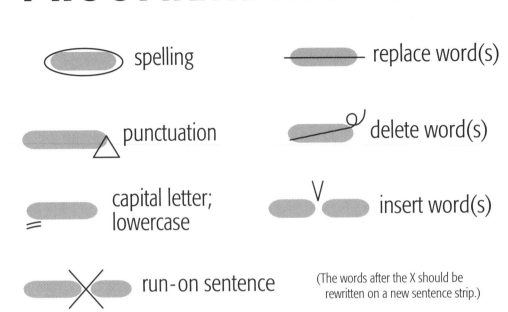

- spelling
- replace word(s)
- punctuation
- delete word(s)
- capital letter; lowercase
- insert word(s)
- run-on sentence (The words after the X should be rewritten on a new sentence strip.)

(?) what you've written does not make sense

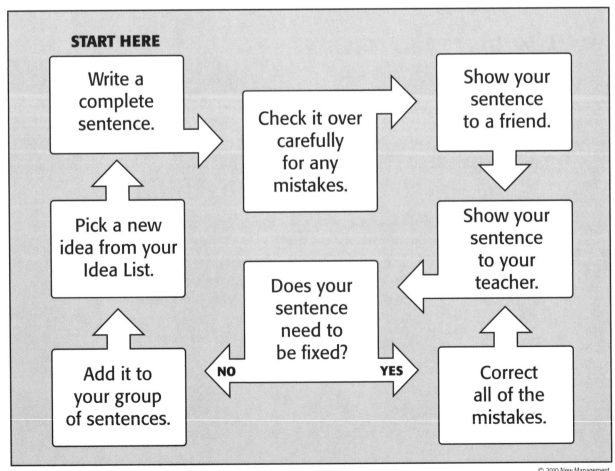

START HERE

Write a complete sentence. → Check it over carefully for any mistakes. → Show your sentence to a friend. ↓

Show your sentence to your teacher.

Does your sentence need to be fixed? — NO / YES

Correct all of the mistakes.

Add it to your group of sentences.

Pick a new idea from your Idea List.

Chapter Six

Core Principles

Confessions of a Former Echoer

The Top Ten Things I Said

Using Music for
Student Independence

Sentence Strips
Cut-and-Paste Paragraphs

Homework Made Easier

Behavior CODES

Credit Cards

*It is the supreme art of the teacher
to awaken joy in creative expression and knowledge.*

—Albert Einstein

Chapter 6
Homework Made Easier

◆ ◆

Goals for this chapter:

☑ Read the latest findings about the effectiveness of homework.

☑ Discover the four keys to making homework easier for you and your students.

☑ Realize the power of a weekly homework bulletin.

☑ Learn simple techniques for record keeping and tracking unfinished assignments.

☑ Put together a powerful program that will make homework effective, yet manageable.

◆ ◆

What's for homework, honey?

Ah, nothin'. I did it at school.

Are you sure?

Yeah, Mom. I'm all done. Can I go play?

Okay, Calvin. Don't stay out too long.

And chalk up another victory for irresponsibility, poor study habits, and ineffective home/school communication. While you're at it, chalk up one more loss for Calvin's academic advancement, accountability, and sense of self-determination.

But who can blame him for attempting to escape his responsibilities? After all, he's only a child, and children are always looking for life's shortcuts. That's their job: to find the path of least resistance. If it comes down to a choice between playing or doing homework, what kid in his right mind is happy grabbing a pencil and cracking his math book?

Homework. The name itself sends stout hearts a-poundin' and weak wills a-swayin'.

Homework. What a drag.

> TEACHER
> *Homework! Yes, Calvin. I said homework. Where is your math assignment? You were supposed to have done it last night and brought it to class today.*

> CALVIN:
> *Oh, I forgot to do it.*

And so it goes and has gone for years on end. Teachers diligently assigning activities for their students to complete at home while these same students diligently work at getting out of them.

I'd say that it's time to rethink things a bit.

Thought One

First of all, it's my feeling that your efforts as an educator to require your students to study at home are worth pursuing. Learning at home can be critically important to your students' overall growth and development. That's assuming, of course, that the assignments are relevant to what you are currently doing in class and within the zone of your students' proximal development.[†]

And, no, it doesn't matter how much you actually do in class during the day; something should be assigned each night—Monday through Thursday—for your students to complete. The concept involved is more than just numbers. In fact, when it comes to learning at home, the following statement is true:

$$370 + 30 > 400$$

It's been shown that the cumulative effect of studying in school for 370 minutes plus studying at home for 30 minutes is greater than just studying in school for 400 minutes. Strange but true; true but strange.

According to the research conducted for the Effective Schools Program, test scores improved *dramatically* when students were exposed to a home learning program.

The researchers studied students who were typically scoring at the 50th percentile on norm-referenced tests of basic skills. They found out that target students who were required to learn and study at home ended up scoring at the 60th percentile.

[†]   Lev Vygotsky, a Russian psychologist, worked extensively on ideas about cognitive development. A part of his legacy is the Zone of Proximal Development, or the gap between what a child can do alone and what he is going to need assistance to do. By keeping assignments and activities just inside of this zone, you're setting the stage for the child to be successful working at home without the need for a parent to act as teacher.

They also discovered that if the teacher not only required homework but consistently collected and evaluated assignments, those same target students rose to the 70th percentile. A twenty-point gain merely because students practiced school at home? That's too great an opportunity to pass up with the "I give them enough to do in class" rationale.

Thought Two

The research I just referenced makes a strong case. At the same time, others out there in the educational world are making a strong case *against* homework and its supposed impact upon achievement. In the interests of fair play, let's listen in on what they are saying. Just bear in mind that someone's arbitrary decision to either include or exclude certain research is bound to have a major influence on the conclusion that is drawn.

Lee Canter, of Assertive Discipline fame and author of *Homework Without Tears*, claims research clearly shows that homework affects a child's achievement. He also says that homework is one of the best way for parents to maintain a day-by-day connection to the school.

Alfie Kohn, author of several books critical of traditional education including *The Homework Myth*, claims there's no evidence that shows homework provides any benefits in elementary school. He also feels it doesn't teach good work habits or develop positive character traits.

Sara Bennett, attorney, activist parent, and author of *The Case Against Homework*, claims that, according to the research, the average amount of homework students are being asked to complete has "skyrocketed" in the past twenty years.

Jay Matthews, writing in the *Washington Post*, claims Kohn and Bennett used incomplete data in their somewhat over-the-top assault on homework and its benefits. Of the inner-city secondary schools showing high achievement that he contacted, all of them had a homework policy.

Harris Cooper, of Duke University and author of *The Battle Over Homework*, looked at more than 100 studies and claims that academic benefits from doing homework show up on standardized tests but only at the secondary level.

Rick Morris, educator and author of several books on effective teaching, claims that if you torture the numbers long enough, you can get them to confess to just about anything.

So, basically, the jury's still out on this one. I've got a couple of comments I'd like to make, though, regarding some of these claims.

Sara Bennett: The research she referred to shows that the homework load for six to eight-year-old children increased from 8 minutes a day in 1981 to 17 minutes a day in 1997. It has since gone up to 22 minutes a day according to a 2003 study. I believe the "skyrocket" she mentioned may have burned out after the first stage.

For high school students, their workload went from 33 minutes in 1981 to 50 minutes in 2003. Apparently they've been talked off the ledge by being allowed to watch TV or use the computer for non-educational activities an average of two-and-a-half hours a day.

Alfie Kohn: In his book, he wonders aloud, "What if, after spending 6 to 7 hours a day at school, we let them have their afternoons and evenings just to be kids?" Here's what I wonder: What does he think those kids are going to do with their extra allotment of 50 minutes? I rather doubt they're going to gather everyone in the family for a game of Parcheesi. It will just be more TV, more video games, more social media, and more texting.

Harris Cooper: He asks, in light of the inconclusive research on academic benefit, that teachers limit homework to 10 minutes per night per grade level. To me, that sounds reasonable. (For more on this, turn to page 124.)

Brian Gill: (I didn't mention him earlier.) Writing for *Theory into Practice*, he said that it's mainly the extreme views that are currently being heard in the homework debate. Opponents overstate the harmful effects while proponents exaggerate the benefits. He'd prefer that we drop the hyperbole and approach the homework issue with a little moderation. Can I get an amen to that, brothers and sisters?

Thought Three

I think that homework, *handled correctly*, can be an effective teaching and learning tool. I also think that homework, *handled poorly*, can be a bigger drag for the teacher than the student. It's the teacher who has to come up with something to do, assign it, spend time in class collecting it, spend more time chasing missing assignments, and spend even more time evaluating it. Wouldn't it be a lot easier to just bag the whole thing?

I suppose. But what are you going to do about those parents—and they are out there—who will begin to bug their kids, and then you, for homework assignments? You can't duck their requests forever. These are the folks who already have the college application forms ready to go even though the child is in second grade. They want to see some tangible evidence that the teacher has high expectations about achievement. For them, homework is a reassuring, hold-it-in-your-hands-and-see-it-with-your-eyes proof that the teacher cares.

So, go ahead and do it the right way. Get organized, get a plan, and use learning at home to your advantage. With the simple recommendations I'm going to offer and the easy-to-use blackline masters found in this chapter, you'll soon begin to see homework as a thing of beauty. (Well, at least not quite such a pain. The beauty part comes later when you see some of your hard-core underachievers begin to blossom and come alive.)

Keys to Success

Homework was an integral part of my classroom program. Some classes proved to be highly successful in regards to homework whereas other classes struggled a bit. That's just how it goes. But, for the most part, I experienced a great deal of success and can point to four simple keys as the reason for most of it.

1. The assignments were manageable for students to complete.

2. The assignments were listed on a weekly bulletin that the students took home and used as a reminder.

3. The students were given time at the end of the day to begin the assignment.

4. The teacher was the one who collected it the next day.

Believe it or not, that's about it. And even though there were certain attitudes I needed to instill in my students and standards I needed to maintain about the actual work being done by the students, the four things listed above really helped to make homework easier and more effective for everyone.

What do you say we take a closer look at each of them?

Key #1: Manageable Assignments

As I reflect on my career as a homework dispenser, I have to say that, for at least 90% of the time, I only assigned one task for my students to take care of each night and return the next day. Whether that assignment was to complete a math activity sheet, write some sentences that included the week's spelling words, answer questions from the social studies book, or complete a family survey, it was always just one thing.

For anyone out there registering panic at the small amount of work I assigned and how it might under-serve the students to ask for so little, allow me to make just one point:

When it comes to homework, the quality of the work they actually do trumps the quantity of the work you assign.

Three or Four Assignments is Too Many

If you regularly assign three or four activities for your students to complete, you might be hindering their ability to do a good job. Let's be realistic. Students only have a set amount of time and energy for completing homework. This is not to disparage their character but to acknowledge that there are other things in their lives that need attention. Being a kid, doing chores, and having dinner are a few of the things. What about piano practice, soccer practice, baseball practice, Girl Scouts, Boy Scouts, and church groups? The cumulative effect can sometimes be greater than we might realize.

When they eventually get around to the four assignments you gave them to complete, they begin to contemplate how quickly it can be done. Any thoughts they may have entertained about doing a quality job have been flattened by the sheer volume of what they're facing.

Quality from Them

W. Edwards Demming, the industrial management guru from the 30's and the pioneer of team-based manufacturing, discovered that if you can cut back on quantity, you'll get quality as a by-product. By assigning just one task to complete and return—decrease the quantity—you will give your students a chance to do a better job—increase the quality.

Take spelling sentences, for example. Teachers have been asking students to write sentences containing their spelling words ever since I was a student. The problem is, most of them go for quantity over quality. By that I mean, if there are 20 words on the spelling list for the week, the students are supposed to write 20 sentences. You can do it that way if you want, but don't be surprised when you see sentences like these:

> I have a bicycle.
> I saw my nephew.
> I like opportunity.

Wake me when it's over.

How about assigning just five sentences to write, and letting them choose the words they're going to include in the sentences?[†] Since they're only having to write five sentences, it would be reasonable for you to request that the sentences be almost poetic in composition. Do that long enough and you'll begin to get sentences that look like these:

> The witch strapped on her dusty apron
> before she stirred her bubbling brew.
> —Gwen DuVall, fifth grade, Class of 1995

> The officer was determined to catch the villains
> who killed Ethan Hunt and the other IMF agents.
> —Robert Milse, third grade, Class of 2000

---

†   For one thing, there's no way your students are going to be able to learn all of the words by merely writing sentences that contain those words. For another, I dare anyone to learn 20 new words a week. I know I couldn't.

Quality From You

Let's back up a bit and look at the other side of the four assignment coin. Your side. Assigning four tasks for your students to complete at home is only one part of the "homework equals success" equation. A second part is whether or not you actually collect them all. *Important:* If you assign four things to complete, then you must collect all four things from each student or you will eventually undermine your own program.

That's a lot of stuff to track down and a lot of papers to keep organized. It's also a lot of work that needs to be evaluated because your evaluation of the assignment represents the third part of the equation. If any of these three parts are missing from the equation, the result is going to be, "Does not equal."

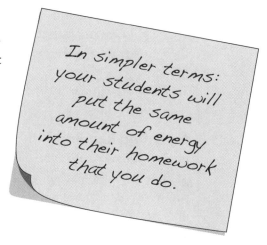

If you don't assign it, they can't do it. If you don't collect it, they'll stop doing it. And if you don't evaluate them and get them back to the students so they can see how they've done, they're going to be less inclined to put much effort into doing a good job in the first place.

In simpler terms: Your students will put the same amount of energy into their homework that you do.

However, if you cut down on the number of assignments and assign just one task, you're more likely to stay on top of both the collection *and* the evaluation. The predictable outcome: They will more consistently complete the assignment and with a higher degree of quality.

Extending Homework

For parents who might want to complain about the light work load, there are two ways to go, both of which I used over the years.

> **Assign weekly tasks to complete:**
>> It would be easy for you to come up with simple things your students could be doing on their own during the week. Depending upon your grade level you could have them:
>> > study the weekly spelling words every night
>> > read for 10-15 minutes every night
>> > maintain a reading log of nightly reading that is due on Friday
>> > practice math facts for the next day's math facts quiz
>> > work on long-term projects that aren't due for several weeks

As you can see, the list can be an extensive one.

Talk with the parents about their concern:

Mr. Morris
>   Meeting with a couple of concerned parents:
>
> *I understand what you're saying about what seems to be not enough homework. What I'm trying to do, by assigning one task to complete each night and return the next day, is instill a sense of pride in workmanship. Besides, if I assigned too many things to complete, it would cut into your family reading time.*
>
>   Puzzled looks from the parents.
>
> *You do have a family reading time each night, don't you? You know, where everyone in the family gathers together and reads silently from a book or magazine?*

They'll get the hint.

Assigning Reading

For last several years in the classroom, I made reading one of the weekly assignments. But not just any kind of reading. I'm talking about pre-reading the next day's lesson. Imagine if you were about to begin a new chapter in your social studies book. It could really boost their understanding if your students were given a chance to read the lesson at home. This kind of "front loading" is especially beneficial for second-language students. That's assuming, of course, that they have the ability to read the material independently.[†]

Key #2: A Weekly Bulletin

One of the best ways to begin to get a handle on the homework issue is to put it in writing. Just about everyone responds to the written word: parents, students, fellow educators, and administrators. A program that is in writing implies dedication, resolve, and forethought. These are good traits to build in your students and, as we all know, one of the strongest teaching messages is contained in what we model. If you want your students to be productive, organized, and on-task, you must exhibit these same behaviors. By putting your homework program on paper, you will be setting the stage for success.

An added bonus is that you will no longer find yourself at the end of the day trying to quickly come up with some kind of assignment for your students to do that night. The entire week's agenda will have been laid out on Monday. That in itself is worth the price of admission.

There are two basic procedures for filling out the actual bulletin. The simple way to go is to fill out the entire sheet yourself. The other way is to just fill out the top part and have your students complete the assignment portion of it. I used both methods over the years. And although they are similar in nature, they met different needs. Let me show you what I mean.

---

† According to the research, 71% of mothers of school-age children are in the work force. *Translation:* Students don't always have the adult assistance available to them that we sometimes think they do.

Teacher Method

If you feel your students are too young to accurately describe their homework activities, feel free to complete the entire bulletin yourself. Along with the basic assignment description, you could include hints and suggestions for successfully completing the various homework activities.

I did this for years with my third graders and enjoyed it immensely; however, I was using a computer and was able to quickly build a new bulletin from the ones I had created in the past.

power
love
fun
freedom
safety

If you do decide to complete it yourself, be careful about the teacher welfare you are generating. Even first graders, bless their little hearts, would welcome the opportunity to help create a bulletin every now and then.

WEEKLY HOMEWORK BULLETIN

Week of: **Oct. 24-28**	**Students of the Week: Rachel Edwards and Mike Quinn**

ELECTION UPDATE

We will be holding elections in Room Twelve on Tuesday. We are looking for someone to be President and someone to be Vice-President. The main duties of office are:

- Attend student council meetings and report details to class
- Greet and assist any and all visitors to our room
- Help Mr. Morris plan and organize special events

If you would like to run for office, please prepare a brief statement as to why you should be elected. You will be able to read your thoughts to the class on Tuesday morning. The actual election will be held at 11:30.

MONDAY NIGHT ❑ Notes on back of bulletin.	**Math Activity Sheet** 1. Complete the sheet. 2. Have someone correct it. 3. Redo incorrect problems.
TUESDAY NIGHT ❑ Notes on back of bulletin.	**Spelling Sentences** 1. Write five creative sentences. 2. Boldface the spelling word. 3. Do not start with I, My, or We.
WEDNESDAY NIGHT ✔ Notes on back of bulletin.	**Social Studies** 1. Answer all of the Check Up questions on page 101. 2. Use words from the question to begin your answer. 3. Answers will be read to the class Thursday morning.
THURSDAY NIGHT ❑ Notes on back of bulletin.	**Practice Spelling Test** 1. Study until you know your words. 2. Have someone give you a test. 3. Rewrite and practice any "study words."

Remember: The best sentences will be added to our book, Hot Stuff!

FIG. 6-2
Although older students can fill in the assignment info, it was kind of fun to do the whole thing myself.

Teacher and Student Method

1. Make a xerox of the blackline master found on page 126. Write the week in the space provided.

2. The space next to it is for special announcements, a focus for the week, student awards, acknowledgements, or whatever you want.

3. Fill the space between the header and the assignment boxes with information about assignments or upcoming classroom/school events.

4. Make copies of your bulletin and distribute to the students on the first day of the school week. As you explain what the homework activities will be for the week, have them write a brief explanation in the spaces provided.

5. Each student then takes home the bulletin to post in some handy place.
    Note: Bulletins do not stay at school stuffed in desks. You might want to spend a moment discussing what to do with it once it gets home.

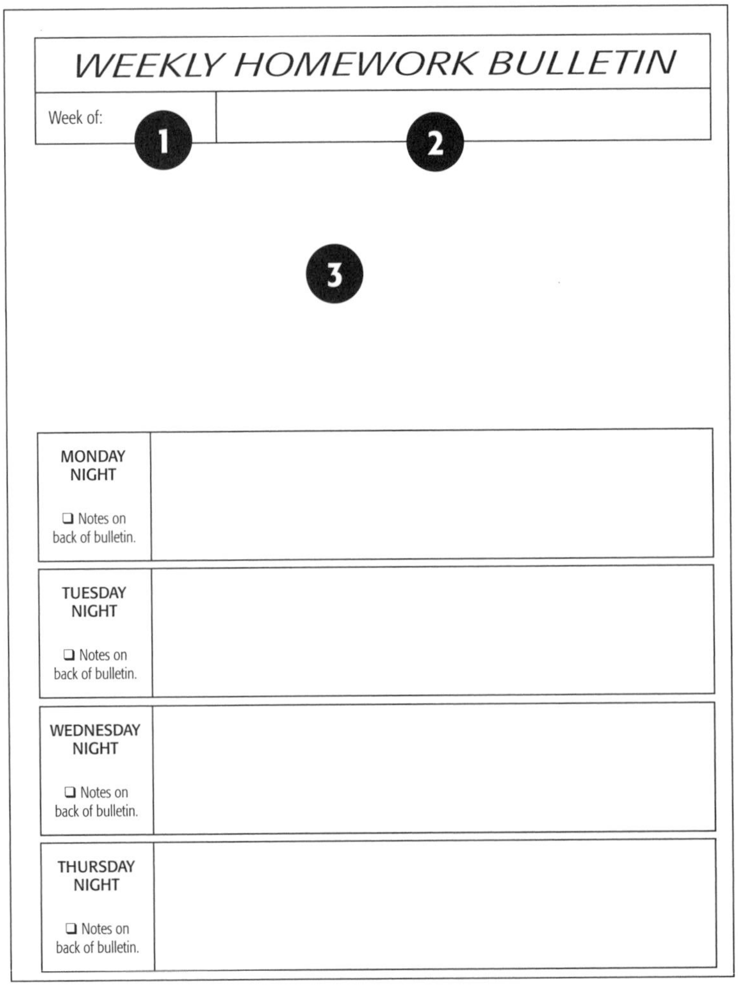

FIG. 6-1
The blackline master for the *Weekly Homework Bulletin* can be found at the end of the chapter.

Additional Suggestions:

> The space next to the "Week of:" box is just right for posting the names of Students of the Week, Honor Roll candidates, or what have you.

> See if you can't include at least one motivational comment on the bulletin each week.

> Including the list of spelling words on the bulletin will eliminate any student from saying, "I can't find my word list."

**power
love
fun
freedom**
safety

> Have a bulletin design contest. Provide your students with the information which needs to be on the next weekly bulletin and see what they come up with. Use the best design as the actual bulletin to be copied and sent home.

"Notes on back of bulletin"

This box can be checked whenever you feel it would be helpful for the students to copy examples or details of how to complete a particular assignment or activity. This makes for an especially powerful addition to your actual lesson.

The teacher-created bulletin on page 113 shows that the students checked this box for Wednesday night's assignment: Social Studies Check Up questions. (Since I wanted my students to develop the skill of introducing their answers with a portion of the question, I felt it would be appropriate to have them write some sample answers on the back of their bulletin.)

If there were six questions to answer altogether, we might have answered the first two in class as examples. Then, when the students were facing Wednesday night's homework, they would have answer models to get them started.

FIG. 6-3
This is a sample of what the students would have written on the back of the bulletin when they received it on Monday.

Q: Why would both New Orleans and Sacramento be considered examples of pluralistic cities?

A: New Orleans and Sacramento would be con- sidered pluralistic cities because they both have people of different backgrounds and ethnic origins living in them.

Important: The note on the back must be completed on Monday before the bulletin goes home for the remainder of the week.

Key #3: *Let Them Begin the Assignment in Class*

Allowing your students to begin their assignment in class—not that they should have enough time to actually complete it— can have a profound impact upon their ultimate success.

1. Students get a chance to "try on" the assignment. Since everyone is a bit leery of the unknown, creating familiarity with the task will take the mystery out of it and replace it with a sense of comfort and safety.

2. Everyone gets a head start. It's just so much easier to complete an assignment you've already begun as opposed to having to start from scratch when you're home alone.

3. Anyone who is confused by the assignment—and they won't know that until they actually begin to work on it—will have an opportunity to ask for help while the teacher is still around. If they take it home and *then realize* they don't know what to do, it's highly likely they'll give up.

4. Since it's one of the last things done before dismissal, it acts as a strong reminder about their accountability for doing the rest of it at home.

So, with about 10 minutes left in our day, I got everyone started on that night's homework. Here are two examples of how I might have put this time to use.

Write 5 Spelling Sentences.
We'd write just one sentence in class. If we had time, we'd allow a few students to read their sentences aloud. By writing just one sentence, I knew my students were heading home with good writing paper, a proper heading on the paper, and a clear understanding of the assignment.

Math Activity Sheet.
I'd assign anywhere from three to five randomly selected problems to complete from the sheet. (Problem numbers 1, 5, 9, 15, and 21 would be a realistic sampling.) After solving and then correcting these five problems in class, the students would be heading home with a fresh review of the necessary skills involved.

Key #4: *The Teacher Collects the Assignments*

Although you could have the students place their assignments in a tote tray or basket, I feel it is most effective if you collect each one personally. When your students know that you will be there each and every day expecting those assignments and activities, it will help them to become more responsible about actually completing them at home.

Homework Grade Book

Before you can collect the first assignment, though, you're going to need a homework grade book. It's actually a folder, but it will help you to keep everything related to homework organized and in one spot. Here's how to make the kind I used.

1. Using the grade sheet blackline master found at the end of this chapter, xerox a copy. Pencil in the first names of your students. Now xerox five or six copies of your new homework grade sheet.

2. Three-hole punch these newly made grade sheets and place them in a folder of some type. *Tip:* Office Depot sells a really nice portfolio (it's called "two-pocket portfolio with fasteners") that makes a perfect grade book. They come in a variety of colors and cost less than a buck.

3. Make an extra copy or two of the Weekly Homework Bulletin and place them in the front pocket of your grade book.

4. Place blackline masters of the weekly bulletin, grade sheet, and the notice about an unfinished assignment in the back pocket.

Since you are now ready to collect the first assignment, I'm going to present three basic techniques for doing so.

Individual Students

After assigning them an independent activity to complete, I began to call students to my desk. Since we used student numbers, I usually called out numbers, five at a time. If you prefer to use names—which will be manageable because you'll have your homework grade book open to the grade sheet where their names are listed—feel free.

MR. MORRIS
Okay. I'm going to start collecting the math activity sheet you did last night. One, two, three, four, five.

Each of these five students brought me his assignment and returned to his seat. I put a little check mark in the upper left hand corner of the grade box to indicate that the student had completed the assignment and a small dot if that wasn't the case.[†] The collected activity sheets were placed in the back of my grade book

HOMEWORK

		TUE 10/25
Ana	1	✓
Angel	2	✓
Ashley	3	✓
Bobby	4	✓
Brianna	5	✓
Calvin	6	•
Christina	7	✓

[†]   I'll address the unfinished assignment procedure on page 120.

behind the grade sheets for later evaluation. I continued calling and collecting until I had seen each student.

power
love
fun
freedom
safety

Recommended: I didn't always go in order, 1 through 30. On some days we went backwards and on other days we'd use the date as a starting point. For example, if the day's date was the 17th, I started with student number 17, worked my way through to number 30, and then collected 1 through 16. Always tried to keep it fresh.

Student Teams

My students were organized in teams with anywhere from 4 to 6 students on a team. Each team was assigned a color of the rainbow to help differentiate one team from another. The colors we used were red, orange, yellow, green, blue, and violet.[†] To help reinforce the team mindset, I sometimes collected assignments by team.

Fig. 6-4
Rainbow Cards are 5 X 8 index cards with colored squares of construction paper glued on them.

Although they don't look like much in this illustration, the effect they created when displayed on the magnetic whiteboard was a powerful one.

To make the whole process easy, I used my Rainbow Cards. (These are nothing more than 5 X 8 index cards with a square of colored construction paper glued to each one. After they'd been laminated, I turned them over and attached a small, self-adhesive magnet.) I just shuffled the cards and slapped them on the whiteboard. Voila! The order in which the teams would come see me had been determined. As opposed to always going in rainbow order, the Rainbow Cards provided a bit of variety, an element of chance, and an overall feeling of playfulness.

As with the technique for individual students, I first assigned everyone an independent activity on which to work and then called up the teams.

Mr. Morris
While you are working on your timelines, I'm going to call you up by teams so that I can collect the map you did last night.
Shuffle, shuffle, shuffle, slap, slap, slap, slap, slap, slap:
Orange Team, please.

The Orange Team, as a group, joined me with their maps. After I had collected all of the maps from the team, they would return to their seats. (I usually encouraged them to remain at my desk until I had dealt with the entire team. This helped to break down the "me habit" and develop the "we habit.")

---

†   When I was teaching third grade with a population of 20 students, we had five teams of four students. We used the first five colors of the rainbow: red, orange, yellow, green, and blue.

As the Orange Team headed back to their pod—our name for their team area—the Blue Team came forward. One of the benefits of using a set of Rainbow Cards was that I only had to call for the first team. After that, the teams were aware of when they were supposed to come see me. I could always count on the fact that *someone* from the Blues would have been watching and waiting for the Oranges to finish and leave.

BLUE TEAM MEMBER
Seeing the Orange Team finish with Mr. Morris:
Come on. It's our turn!

And so it went, color by color, until I had met with all six teams.

Oral Presentations

Many times I found that the assignment was well suited to be presented orally to the class. Spelling sentences were a good example of this.

MR. MORRIS
Wanting to give his students some public speaking experience:
Instead of bringing me your spelling sentences by yourself or with your team, why don't we have everyone read one to the class? Cool idea, huh?

Students could go in numerical order, they could go up as a team, or they could go in random order. If we did it randomly, I'd use a method called Center Stage: a variation on the basic Class Cards technique. (As opposed to my set made from playing cards—durable and fun to shuffle!—the Center Stage set was made with 3 X 5 index cards. Each card had the name of one student on it. Index cards were great because they enabled me to record a simple assessment of the presentations with a plus, check, or minus.)

MR. MORRIS
Shuffling the Center Stage deck:
Take a moment to choose one sentence. Read it over in your head a couple of times.
Shuffle, shuffle, shuffle:
I'm going to call three names. When you hear your name, go to the front of the class-room. All three students will take a turn and read one sentence. After reading to us, place your sentences on my desk and step back. When all three have read, they will have a seat and I'll call three more names.
Shuffle, shuffle, shuffle:
If you don't have your sentences, you will need to go to the front when it's your turn and tell us that.† Okay, here we go. Ramil, Valerie, and Nathan.

By going through all of the cards, everyone was given a fair chance to read. Also, I was guaranteed that no one would have been inadvertently overlooked. Could life get any better?

---

† Although this may seem harsh, it's a part of how my students experienced the consequences of not being responsible. I can promise you, though, that no one was allowed to tease or make fun of the child offering a *mea culpa*.

Late or Unfinished Assignments

There will be times when a student will say that he doesn't have the assignment ready to hand in. There are as many different reasons for this as there are days in the school year. What I usually did was bypass the excuse being offered and proceeded directly to a basic "yes or no" line of questioning. I wanted my students to realize that stories did not take the place of the actual assignment required. Unfortunately, most of them had learned at home that a good excuse would get them out of most difficulties.

> MR. MORRIS
> *Do you have your assignment, Calvin?*

> CALVIN
> *Well, no. You see, we went bowling last night and...*

> MR. MORRIS
> Calmly:
> *Calvin. Yes or no, do you have your assignment?*

> CALVIN
> *No.*

> MR. MORRIS:
> *Please fill out this form and bring it back tomorrow with your spelling sentences.*

Calvin received a Notice of Unfinished Assignment form to fill out and take home and I placed a little dot—not finished—in my grade book. (See facing page.)

And the next day, when I was collecting a new homework assignment, the dot in the box would alert me to the fact that Calvin should be returning his Notice of Unfinished Assignment along with the assignment. I found that compliance and accountability went up dramatically when I consistently followed up on late work. By week three or four, I usually saw a significant increase in the number of completed activities being returned to class on time.

In fact, many parents had told me that within a month or so they no longer had to "battle with their children over homework." Their children—my students—knew what was expected of them and that I would be there the next day with my hand out. And even though it wasn't always fun to do the work at home, it was a great feeling for them to be able to hand in a completed assignment and receive a "well done" in return.

FIG. 6-5
The black-line master for the *Notice of Unfinished Assignment* can be found at the end of the chapter.

Homework

Notice of Unfinished Assignment

Name Calvin   Date Oct. 26

Assignment spelling sentences

I will complete this learning activity tonight and return it to class on the next school day.

Calvin
Student signature

_____
Parent signature

Grade Keeping

Here are a few suggestions for making the record keeping process a manageable one.

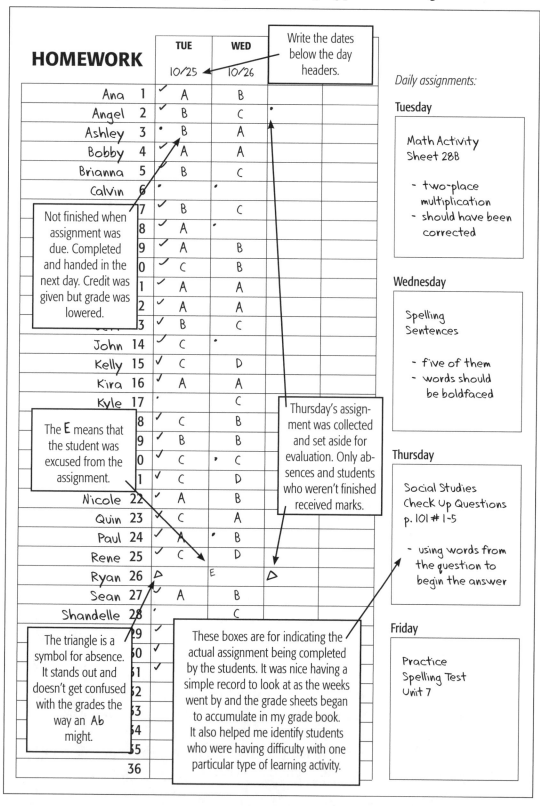

HOMEWORK

Write the dates below the day headers.

		TUE 10/25	WED 10/26	
Ana	1	✓ A	B	
Angel	2	✓ B	C	•
Ashley	3	• B	A	
Bobby	4	✓ A	A	
Brianna	5	B	C	
Calvin	6	•	•	
	7	✓ B	C	
	8	✓ A	•	
	9	✓ A	B	
	0	✓ C	B	
	1	✓ A	A	
	2	✓ A	A	
	3	✓ B	C	
John	14	✓ C	•	
Kelly	15	✓ C	D	
Kira	16	✓ A	A	
Kyle	17	•	C	
	8	✓ C	B	
	9	✓ B	B	
	0	✓ C	• C	
	1	✓ C	D	
Nicole	22	✓ A	B	
Quin	23	✗ C	A	
Paul	24	✓ A	• B	
Rene	25	✓ C	D	
Ryan	26	◿	E	◿
Sean	27	✓ A	B	
Shandelle	28	•	C	
	29	✓		
	30	✓		
	31	✓		
	32			
	33			
	34			
	35			
	36			

Not finished when assignment was due. Completed and handed in the next day. Credit was given but grade was lowered.

The **E** means that the student was excused from the assignment.

The triangle is a symbol for absence. It stands out and doesn't get confused with the grades the way an **Ab** might.

Thursday's assignment was collected and set aside for evaluation. Only absences and students who weren't finished received marks.

These boxes are for indicating the actual assignment being completed by the students. It was nice having a simple record to look at as the weeks went by and the grade sheets began to accumulate in my grade book. It also helped me identify students who were having difficulty with one particular type of learning activity.

Daily assignments:

Tuesday

Math Activity Sheet 28B

- two-place multiplication
- should have been corrected

Wednesday

Spelling Sentences

- five of them
- words should be boldfaced

Thursday

Social Studies Check Up Questions p. 101 # 1-5

- using words from the question to begin the answer

Friday

Practice Spelling Test Unit 7

FIG. 6-6
It may look like sanscrit right now, but you'll soon be able to read it like the TV guide.

Homework Journals

When I said earlier that one of the keys to making homework more successful was to put the actual assignment information in writing, I didn't mean that it had to be limited to the Weekly Homework Bulletin you read about. Journals are another great way to put things in writing so that the students know what they need to be doing that night.

When we finally got a decent printer in my classroom, I started to type up the assignments on a daily basis. I would then cut-and-paste the text so I ended up with four blocks of text on a single sheet of paper. By printing 5 copies and then cutting them apart on the paper cutter, I would end up with 20 quarter-page homework notices. I would pass them out at the end of the day and the students would glue-stick-it on one of their journal pages.

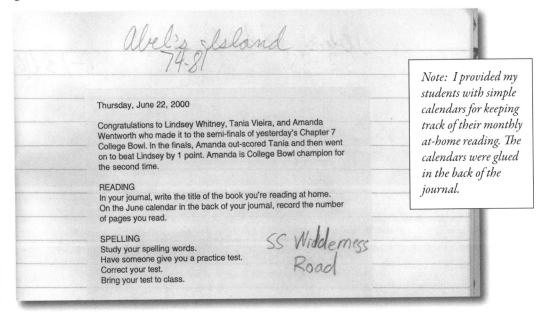

FIG. 6-7
Here's an inside view of the Homework Journal with the night's homework note glued to the page.

Thursday, June 22, 2000

Congratulations to Lindsey Whitney, Tania Vieira, and Amanda Wentworth who made it to the semi-finals of yesterday's Chapter 7 College Bowl. In the finals, Amanda out-scored Tania and then went on to beat Lindsey by 1 point. Amanda is College Bowl champion for the second time.

READING
In your journal, write the title of the book you're reading at home. On the June calendar in the back of your journal, record the number of pages you read.

SPELLING
Study your spelling words.
Have someone give you a practice test.
Correct your test.
Bring your test to class.

Note: I provided my students with simple calendars for keeping track of their monthly at-home reading. The calendars were glued in the back of the journal.

One advantage to using typed daily notices was that I was able to adjust the assignments as the week progressed. Another advantage was the ability to write a note in the journal for the parents to see. It was kind of fun to get into a little back-and-forth comment sharing as the week went by.

The disadvantage to using the journal as opposed to the weekly bulletin was having to remember to do the day's notice before dismissal. It sometimes got to be a bit of a frenzy.

Weekly bulletin or student journal? It doesn't matter. The important thing is that the homework assignments are being recorded on paper for everyone to see.

Informing the Parents

Here's a copy of the letter I sent home to the parents at the beginning of the year. It briefly detailed the homework program and, more importantly, let them know that they could expect to see a Weekly Homework Bulletin coming home every Monday for the remainder of the year.

From the desk of Mr. Morris

Dear Parents,

Homework can be a critical part of a sound education. The three basic purposes of homework are to review material taught at school, to encourage independence and creativity, and to promote academic growth and development. According to *What Works*, the United States Department of Education's survey of research on good learning and teaching practices, "Student achievement rises significantly when teachers regularly assign homework and students conscientiously do it."

To help with the "regularly assign homework" aspect of the study, I've created a Weekly Homework Bulletin. This assignment sheet, sent home every Monday, will contain information about the week's home learning activities. (These activities will also be explained before your child leaves at the end of the school day. Every effort will be made to ensure that the students are heading home with a clear understanding of what is required that night. Any child is welcomed—encouraged, actually—to seek additional directions or clarification of any aspect of homework.) When a student and his parents understand the assignments, working successfully at home can become a reality.

Although homework is essentially a contract between teacher and student, all children work better when they know their parents are interested. While you should not "study" for your child or do his assignments, you can provide a helpful home atmosphere which encourages your child to do his best.

Please feel free to get in touch with me if you have any questions or concerns regarding your child's home learning activities. I think it is through this kind of cooperation that homework can become the teaching and learning tool it was meant to be.

Sincerely,

Mr. Morris

Some Final Thoughts

Education is a process

Be patient with your students. Your new homework program might be totally new and unexpected. So if, in the beginning, you get a bit of resistance, just continue assigning and collecting in a calm, consistent fashion. Some of them are just checking to see if you're serious. With time—two months?—they'll come to realize that you mean business and their attitudes will show some real progress.

How Much Should You Assign?

Back on page 108, Harris Cooper, author of *The Battle Over Homework*, suggested that 10 minutes per night per grade would be an appropriate measuring stick to use when trying to determine how much homework should be assigned. Nonetheless, what might take one student 20 minutes to complete could take another student an hour or more. So, realistically, it's hard to come up with a one-size-fits-all standard. Just be sensitive to the needs of your students and the difficulty of your assignments.

Something else to keep in mind is that the one assignment they've been asked to complete is only one part of the homework. My students, for example, also knew to read for 10-15 minutes, study a handful of spelling words, and practice whatever multiplication fact family we happened to be working on that week. It could add up quickly if I wasn't careful.

Massed Practice (quantity) vs Distributive Practice (quality)

John Rosemond, a family psychologist and author of *Ending the Homework Hassle*, has identified one of the main problems with the traditional homework philosophy: more is better. There's no need to ask your students to do 50 tough subtraction problems—massed practice—when doing 10 problems over the course of two days—distributive practice—is not only psychologically more attractive but a more effective way to reinforce the skill. When teachers engage in massed practice, the main thing students learn is, "Homework is painful and should be avoided whenever possible."

Suggestion: If you're going to have your students complete a math activity sheet for homework, just assign the even-numbered problems. This provides you with three immediate advantages.

1. It will be obvious to your students that, although you could have assigned all of the problems, you've only asked that they do half of them. They'll appreciate this.
2. It will be easier for you to correct the assignment after you've collected them all. (I can't emphasize how important this part of the process is. See next page, Evaluate and Share.)
3. If a child requires more help to master the skill being practiced, you'll be able to use the odd-numbered problems during your reteaching session. You won't have to search around for a comparable set of problems.

Hold Off on the *Unfinished Assignment Notice*

Since you're going to be exercising patience, you might want to wait a month or so before you begin to use the notice about an unfinished assignment. Give your students a chance to work it out on their own without Mom or Dad jumping into the fray. If, however, your generosity is being abused or ignored, crack out the notices and send 'em home.

Fun Stuff

power
love
fun
freedom
safety

Assign a non-academic activity every few weeks. Bringing in supplies for an art project, a snack for a special activity, or an item they can't get at school (a stamped, addressed envelope for mailing a friendly letter we're going to write in class) are a few simple examples. There are lots of possibilities which will help to lighten their load and maintain their enthusiasm.

Spelling Words

Since so many of my students had a difficult time holding on to their spelling take-home lists, we usually added our spelling words to the bulletin. Since Thursday night's assignment was almost always a practice spelling test, I learned to include the words in the Thursday Night space. Another way to go would be to have the students complete a spelling pre-test on the back of the weekly bulletin before it went home.

Evaluate and Share

You need to make sure you are checking and evaluating these assignments. The effort they put into their activities is directly related to the effort you put into them. If you're just collecting them but not evaluating and sharing the results with the students, the quality of what they're producing will eventually become rather sad and pathetic.

Recommended: Only assign tasks you plan to collect and evaluate.

Tips for Parents (page 129)

At the end of this chapter, hiding just behind the three blackline masters to be used for organizing your homework program, is a *Tips for Parents* sheet. I thought you might find it helpful to have something to send home to the folks. It's basically a one-page condensation of several volumes worth of information about the issue of homework and how parents can help to make it the powerhouse learning tool it is supposed to be.

The Bulletin Habit

It takes a bit of time to get into the habit of having the weekly homework bulletin ready to go Monday morning. But once you have it down, you'll truly enjoy the freedom of not having to worry about one of your students asking, "What's for homework?"

Ah, sweet relief.

WEEKLY HOMEWORK BULLETIN

Week of:

MONDAY NIGHT	
❏ Notes on back of bulletin.	

TUESDAY NIGHT	
❏ Notes on back of bulletin.	

WEDNESDAY NIGHT	
❏ Notes on back of bulletin.	

THURSDAY NIGHT	
❏ Notes on back of bulletin.	

HOMEWORK

	TUE	WED	THUR	FRI
1				
2				
3				
4				
5				
6				
7				
8				
9				
10				
11				
12				
13				
14				
15				
16				
17				
18				
19				
20				
21				
22				
23				
24				
25				
26				
27				
28				
29				
30				
31				
32				
33				
34				
35				
36				

Daily assignments:

Tuesday

Wednesday

Thursday

Friday

Homework

Notice of Unfinished Assignment

Name   Date

Assignment

*I will complete this
learning activity tonight
and return it to class
on the next school day.*

_____
Student signature

_____
Parent signature

Homework

Notice of Unfinished Assignment

Name   Date

Assignment

*I will complete this
learning activity tonight
and return it to class
on the next school day.*

_____
Student signature

_____
Parent signature

Homework

Notice of Unfinished Assignment

Name   Date

Assignment

*I will complete this
learning activity tonight
and return it to class
on the next school day.*

_____
Student signature

_____
Parent signature

Homework

Notice of Unfinished Assignment

Name   Date

Assignment

*I will complete this
learning activity tonight
and return it to class
on the next school day.*

_____
Student signature

_____
Parent signature

Tips for Parents

Homework Matters

According to the *What Works* study, homework can have a positive impact on student learning. And although homework is essentially a contract between the teacher and the student, there are certain things parents can do to help make homework more successful.

❖ Don't Do the Work for Your Child

Homework is designed to help the child improve academic skills. When the assignment is done by the parent, no learning occurs other than, "My parents will do my work for me." Also, your child's teacher will have a false impression of his skills when the work being turned in is not his own. So, be a supervisor and not an assistant. Make yourself available to offer advice or to help clarify instructions. But, as much as possible, avoid the temptation to take over.

❖ Establish a Study Area

Research has shown that not everyone works well in the same environment. Although some children enjoy listening to music as they complete assignments, others would rather have things as quiet as possible. As opposed to insisting that one style is better than another, take the time to discuss with your child what works best. Make sure you cover important issues such as privacy, lighting, furniture needs, etc. By collaborating on the study area, your child will view it in a more positive way.

❖ Decide on a Schedule

Similar to the study area issue above, scheduling a time to work on homework should be negotiated instead of imposed. A reasonable option would be that your child completes the homework before dinner. This will allow him a chance to go play for a bit and get rid of some pent-up energy. If, however, your child is not abiding by your agreed upon schedule, it will be your responsibility to enforce a less flexible one in which he is allowed fewer choices.

❖ Be an Encourager

Taking an interest in the assignment and the way your child is working on it will encourage him to stay on task. Knowing that his parents care about homework will help him to care about it.

❖ Get it Back to School

It's never good for a child to begin the school day by having to tell the teacher that he forgot to bring his homework to class. Help your child figure out a plan for what to do with the finished assignments so that they do get back to school. And, as much as possible, give your child the responsibility for following the plan.

What to do when...

My child refuses to do his homework. We fight about it every day.
Although talking with your child should be enough, some children need to see that you mean what you say. Robert MacKenzie, author of *Setting Limits*, suggests that parents present their children with choices. "You have a choice. You can do your homework without complaining, or you can lose your privileges." The key is to keep everything calm and under control. And if your child still refuses? Take away the privileges. To children, action is the only reality. When parents don't back up their words, children learn to ignore them.

My child sometimes says that he did his homework at school.
"I already did it," is just one of the many ways in which children try to manipulate their parents. Make an agreement with your child that he will bring home his assignment every day, finished or not. This will remove the temptation to avoid the work by saying that it was done at school.

It seems as if my child always waits until the last minute to get his assignment done.
Learning how to schedule your time properly is something everyone has to learn. To help your child overcome the bad habit of putting things off, show him how to make a weekly calendar. Have him write his responsibilities on the calendar so that the proper time can be devoted to each item. Sometimes just seeing how busy the days are can motivate a child to work ahead instead of always working behind.

Even though my child does his homework, it's always sloppy.
Children will get away with whatever they can get away with. Your child needs to know that you have expectations of quality that will not be compromised. Requiring your child to redo an assignment because it was sloppy will help him understand that you are serious about your expectations.
"If you don't want to redo it, make sure you do a good job the first time."

References

Bennett, S. & Kalish, N. (2006). The case against homework: How homework is hurting our children and what we can do about it. New York, NY: Crown

Canter, L. (2005). Homework without tears. New York, NY: Collins

Cooper, H. (2001). The battle over homework: An administrator's guide to setting sound and effective policies (2nd ed.). Thousand Oaks, CA: Corwin Press

Gill, B.P. (2004). Villain or savior? The American discourse on homework, 1850-2003. Theory Into Practice - Volume 43, Number 3, Summer 2004, pp. 174-181

Kohn, A. (2006). The homework myth: Why our kids are getting too much of a bad thing. Cambridge, MA: De Capo Press

Matthews, J. (2006, November 21). The weak case against homework. Washington Post

MacKenzie, R. (2003). Setting limits in the classroom: How to move beyond the dance of discipline in today's classrooms. (2nd ed.). Roseville, CA: Prima Publishing

Rosemond, J. (1990). Ending the homework hassle. Kansas City, MO: Andrews and Mc-Meel

Chapter Seven

Core Principles

Confessions of a Former Echoer

The Top Ten Things I Said

Using Music for
Student Independence

Sentence Strips
Cut-and-Paste Paragraphs

Homework Made Easier

Behavior CODES

Credit Cards

Pick battles big enough to matter,
but small enough to win.

—Jonathon Kozol

Chapter 7
Behavior CODES

◆ ◆

Goals for this chapter:

☑ Understand that classes and their needs differ from one year to the next.

☑ Learn about a simple intervention for dealing with social talking.

☑ Discover how to modify the social talking intervention to deal with other issues.

☑ Create an easy-to-use seating chart coding system for documenting misbehavior.

☑ Learn how a powerful grade-keeping program can create behavior bulletins.

◆ ◆

Around year twenty of my career I had a class that was a handful and a half. One of those sad situations in which it felt as if there were more negative students than positive ones. I'm not saying it's true; but, it sure felt that way.

I would barely have a fire contained in one part of the room only to see a new one flare up someplace else. (Or three someplace elses, if you know what I mean.) By the end of our first month together, I finally accepted the fact that my little bucket of water was not going to get the job done. Not when the whole neighborhood was in flames.

So, I decided that this class was in need of something a bit more drastic. And that, in itself, is an important lesson for teachers: every class is different, and you've got to adapt to their differences. The strategies you've employed quite successfully with compliant classes might not produce the same results with the tough class you now have.

It can be frustrating to recall the previous years when you had your students on board the Classroom Happy Bus, singing camp songs as you rolled through Learning Land. Just cruisin' along, year after year, doin' a great job, lovin' school, loved and adored by your students. You were even beginning to think, "Hey, I wonder if I've got a shot at our district's Teacher of the Year award?" when, to your dismay, you get your new class and, before you know it, they've not only hijacked the bus, they've thrown you under it.

A bit dramatic, I confess, but the situation is not uncommon. Here I had been feeling great; doing what I thought was a good job of teaching. Then the new school year started and, lo and behold, I realized I had been assigned the cast from *Lord of the Flies.*

The double whammy with this new group was the high number of students who didn't seem to care about being responsible and the variety of ways in which they manifested this irresponsibility. The five misbehaviors I had to deal with the most produced the acronym ADOPT: the name of the discipline strategy I created that year.[†]

> **A** = not paying **A**ttention
>
> **D** = not following **D**irections
>
> **O** = not staying **O**n task
>
> **P** = **P**laying around (Self-Control on the progress report)
>
> **T** = not completing assignments on **T**ime

Now then, if these five don't match the concerns you have about your own class, don't despair. The ADOPT program will work with a variety of misbehaviors, not just the five shown above. Maybe social talking, to take just one example, is your hot button issue.

Honestly, I wouldn't be surprised if it is.

Social Talking

According to the research, social talking (ST) represents about 80% of off-task behavior in today's classrooms. These neighbor-to-neighbor dialogues about anything *but* what the students should be focused on robs them of valuable learning time.

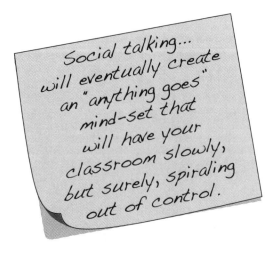

Social talking... will eventually create an "anything goes" mind-set that will have your classroom slowly, but surely, spiraling out of control.

And not only does social talking produce a reduction in time spent on task, it also begins to exert a subtle, yet significant, impact upon the students' perception of your classroom standards. Social talking that is either ignored, or in any other way mishandled, will eventually create an "anything goes" mind-set that will have your classroom slowly, but surely, spiraling out of control.

So, let's take a moment and look more closely at the issue of social talking and use it as a model for how to address just about any type of misbehavior. Because, generally speaking, misbehavior is misbehavior. It doesn't matter what form it takes. What matters is that you deal with it effectively.

---

†   I no longer recommend using ADOPT as the name of this program. The overall strategy of using behavior codes is still as effective as ever. However, the acronym ADOPT needs to be dropped. I'll explain why in just a bit.

Recommended: If social talking is not your big issue, feel free to substitute your own issue—"My students don't listen to me during lessons."—whenever you see the words *social talking* or the initials *ST*.

What Do I Do?

Well, let's start with what *not* to do.

Talk About It

You can't just talk to your students about social talking being an issue. Besides the irony of the teacher talking about students talking, words alone will have little effect on some students. (This point was introduced back on page 6 in the piece about Core Principle #2: Your words equal your actions.) They've learned to tune out an adult's words because there is very rarely any action behind the words. To students, the talk is just something to be tolerated until it stops.

Remember the old Peanuts cartoon specials? Instead of hearing the voice of Charlie Brown's mother, who was forever off-stage, you would hear the sound of a trombone making a kind of drawn out *waa-waa-waa* sound. To many students, it's pretty much the same thing.

Children learn in fundamentally different ways than do adults.

—Jean Piaget

> OLD SCHOOL TEACHER
> Trying to address the issue of social talking:
> *"Waa waa waa waa waa waa waa* **talking** *waa waa waa waa* **stop** *waa waa waa waa* **right now**. *Waa waa waa."*

The fact that students often ignore a teacher's repeated reminders and warnings is nothing more than a product of how students learn appropriate behavior in the first place. Jean Piaget, briefly mentioned on page 6, was a pioneer in the field of child development. He discovered that children learn in fundamentally different ways than do adults. For the most part, the world of children is primarily the world of actions and experiences. It's not *what they hear* that affects their behavior. It's *what happens to them* as a result of their behavior that has an impact.

> *In a nutshell:* Touch the stove, burn your finger, lesson learned: touching the stove is not worth a blistered finger. Talk to your neighbor, get an earful of grief from your teacher but nothing else, lesson learned: talking to my neighbor is worth the nuisance of a short lecture from the teacher.

Granted, there will be a small handful of students who will cease ST in response to the teacher's admonishments. Unfortunately, though, this is almost counter-productive. Since the teacher received reinforcement that talking to the class will cure the ill—after all, some of the students *did* cease—the teacher assumes that words will fix the problem with everyone else. Thus, the lectures—now with an extra shot of volume and a twist of anger—continue.

Compounding the whole mess is the Old School shotgun approach most teachers employ in these situations.

But we're talking about some hardcore, willful students who are able to dismiss words as empty vessels with little or no meaning. These students have made a living out of not listening to adults. And although this all started in the home with their parents, it is now being applied in the classroom with their teachers.

Therefore, if the teacher is all words but no actions—just like good ol' Mom and Dad, or Mom and Step-Dad, or Grandma because Dad is in prison and Mom has run off to Vegas[†]—students learn to ignore the words and the social talking continues unabated.

Compounding the whole mess is the Old School shotgun approach most teachers employ in these situations. It's the "blast everyone" kind of a deal. (This was mentioned on page 10 in regard to Core Principle #4: You can focus your attention.) Even though some of the students no longer engage in ST, they are still subjected to the same rant and rage that is being directed to the non-compliers. However, when teachers speak to the entire class about the actions of a few—which teachers have been doing forever with very little effect—they are actually conditioning their students to tune out the message.

FED-UP TEACHER
Raging about the non-stop social talking:
Hey! What did I say about all of the talking in here? If I have to start calling parents then maybe I'll waa waa waa waa waa waawaa waa waawaa waa waa waa waawaa waa waa waa waa waa waawaa waa waawaa waa waa waa waawaa!

NON-SOCIAL TALKING STUDENT
With a turned-aside head, heavy heart, and slowly closing ears:
*[Man, I hate it when teachers do this. Blah, blah, blah. Hey, dude.
Either shut-up or do something about it. I am so done with this...]*

---

†   Please don't misconstrue this as an insensitive statement about student families. I've just learned, from experience, not everyone grew up with the same stable home situation I did. It's been proven, though, that teachers have a tendency to project their own life experience onto their students. This can lead to feelings of disappointment, frustration, and even resentment when a student doesn't deal with an issue in the same way that the teacher would have at that age. As a student, you would have never considered ignoring your teacher's requests by continuing to engage in the social talking that triggered the requests. So, since you wouldn't have done that when you were a student, it's going to bother you that your own students do not have the same standards or values. And that's the part that leads to the frustration which, in turn, produces the negatively-charged emotional reactions.

And off he goes into some little mental safe house to weather the storm of harsh words. In a desperate attempt to escape—which is nothing more than emotional self-defense— he's learning to hide within an invisible shell of protection. Before too long, he finds that he's actually happier there than in the somewhat hostile environment of a misbehaving class. The predictable outcome? He is now tuning out not just the harsh words but the important ones as well.

Try To Ignore It

You can't just ignore the social talking and hope that it's going to go away on its own. For the most part, misbehavior that is ignored will only get worse. And the worse it gets, the more the class spins out of control. With time, the teacher loses the support of even the normally compliant students, something no one can afford to do.

Reality: Every classroom has its predictable populations of students. You've got your small group of positive students. You've also got your small group of assertive, willful non-compliers. But the largest group is almost always the fence sitters: the undecided voters who could swing either way. In a classroom where the teacher is not able to effectively deal with negative behavior, the fence sitters will eventually slip to the Dark Side. And when that happens, it's lights out.[†]

If, on the other hand, your words and actions do eliminate the misbehavior, you will convince the fence sitters to go the right way. This will tip the balance in the room, and the whole class will begin to swing the right way.

So, regardless of how you actually respond to ST—or whatever misbehavior you chose as the substitute issue—you must always consider those three groups.

STUDENT GROUPS	
The Positives:	*Need your support and encouragement.*
The Negatives:	*Need your intervention.*
The Fence Sitters:	*Need to be convinced that it's better to join the Positives.*

That's not to say that you need to deal with them in the order they are listed. In fact, I'd recommend that you first come to grips with the negatives. This on its own will have a dramatic impact upon the fence sitters since a few of them will not require that much encouragement to go the right way.

Then, as the negative climate has begun to improve, it will become easier to switch the focus to the more positive students which will actually benefit everyone.

---

† One of the main reasons the fence sitters will align themselves with the knuckleheads has to do with those important student needs, power and safety. If they perceive that the negative students have all of the power, they will most likely slide over to their camp. Everyone wants to feel as if they are a part of a group, especially if the group is the dominant one. In a primal way, this feels safe. It's human nature on a very basic, almost genetic, level.

What To Do

So, you can't talk about it. Neither can you just ignore it. Now what? (And, remember, our focus is social talking but it could be any of a number of misbehaviors.)

A Sign for Quiet

Another Old School response to social talking is a raised hand that is supposed to be a signal to the students that the teacher would like it to be quiet. Almost painful to watch, it takes a committed individual to use this technique effectively. However, if it works in your room, have at it. Using a sign is a win-win because: 1) it's a non-verbal cue, and 2) it involves the students as part of the solution.

But what do you do when you don't have the visual attention of your students? How long do you plan to stand there with your hand raised as you wait for the ST to stop? You could be there a while, because if you give in and lower your hand even though some students are still talking, you're basically conceding defeat. And the next time you raise your hand, it might as well be holding a white flag.

A Sound for Quiet

If you feel a signal is a good way to go, I recommend that you try an auditory signal. Find a simple sound maker you can use to indicate to your students that you want any and all ST to cease. (I've used a dog squeak toy and a little dog obedience clicker[†].) The sound you generate will cut through the noise and alert even the talkers that they need to stop.

Unfortunately, though, we're right back to an Old School shotgun approach. Talkers *and* non-talkers hear the click. Too much clicking could begin to produce feelings of resentment and revenge.

Of even more significance is this: What is your plan for dealing with the students who do not stop the ST after you've clicked?

Act On It

Although it is sometimes unpleasant to think about having to act upon your expectations of appropriate behavior—"Why can't they just stop talking when I ask them to?"—it's really the only thing that works with some students. And once you realize how easy it is to do *and* how effective it actually is, you'll convince yourself it's the best way to go.

Before you decide on the action to take, you need to first determine how pervasive the problem is. Is it just a couple of students who are not being compliant, or is it ten to

---

†   I sometimes used my clicker during oral reading sessions to indicate we needed a student to read the next passage. A single *click* told the current reader to select someone to take over.

twenty of them who are pushing your buttons? Since I'm going to give you a strategy for both situations, we might as well start with the simple intervention. After that, I'll show you how easy it is to take on a whole group of non-compliers.

Yellow Slips for Social Talkers

Actions that include some type of documentation send a strong message. Also, keeping a written record will provide you with the information you need so that you can begin to focus your attention on which students are in greatest need of intervention.

The form shown below is called a yellow slip. That's because, although you can't see it here, it's been xeroxed on yellow paper. By using a color—and, no, it doesn't have to be yellow—you're providing yourself with a convenient "handle" for the form itself. It's just easier to say, "Please fill out this yellow slip," as opposed to, "Please fill out this form regarding social talking and what you should have been doing instead of talking socially with the person to whom you were talking." "Yellow slip" worked in my classroom and is what I'll be using for the remainder of this section. As with most of the ideas I share, though, it's up to you.

A Reminder About Staying On Task

Name/#: _____   Date: ____ / ____ / ____

I was talking to _____ instead of:

___   participating in the lesson

___   working on my assignment

___   working with my group

___   reading independently

___   _____

☐ student comments on back   ☐ teacher comments on back

FIG. 7-1
The blackline master for the yellow slip can be found on the last page of this chapter.

A Word to Secondary Teachers

Yellow slips can work for you. I'd recommend that you try it out on just one of your many different groups of students. And since you're only going to start with one period,

I suggest you choose your favorite period. This will most likely be the group with whom you not only have the best relationship, but also experience the least amount of off-task behavior. By starting with your most compliant class, you won't need to pass out too many yellow slips which will help you get off to an easier start.

Also, whenever I mention "at recess" or "at lunch," merely substitute the words, "at the end of the period."[†]

Introducing Yellow Slips to Your Students

power
love
fun
freedom
safety

Since it's rarely a good idea to surprise your students with some new discipline strategy, I recommend you introduce yellow slips to your students at some point. The beginning of the day—or period—when they're all still relatively compliant would be good.

> Mr. Morris
>> Having given each student a yellow slip:
>>> *The little piece of paper in your hand is called a yellow slip. I'm going to use these when students are talking to their neighbors instead of being on task.*
>> Pausing to allow that to sink in:
>>> *As you can see, it's an easy form to fill out. In fact, why don't we practice filling out a yellow slip?*
>> Pausing again to allow the slight panic of the positives to abate:
>>> *This is just for practice. It's not going to count against you. Calm down.*
>> A smile and then:
>>> *Find the space for your name and number. Write your first name on the line and then your student number. You can use cursive or print. It doesn't matter.*

Important point: If I were to see students looking at their neighbors for clarification of what I thought was a rather simple request, I'd say, "If you'd like a sample, just ask." This would mean, of course, that I had an easy way to model for them. Having a projected copy of the yellow slip—say, one placed under a document camera—would able them to see the actual form you're talking about and watch you fill in the blanks.

> Mr. Morris
>> *For the date, you need to write the numbers for the month, day, and year. What would those numbers be?*

> Student
>> *10, 4, 06.*

> Mr. Morris
>> *Thanks. Anyone else?*

[†] I feel it's okay to hold certain students back for a minute before releasing them. And even though I understand their need to get to their next class on time, someone has got to hold them accountable for their misbehavior. For any student who wants to whine about needing to leave at the bell, just let them know, "*When* you engage in social talk, *then* you leave late. If you don't want to leave late, don't engage in social talk." Enough said.

STUDENT 2
> *It's 10, 4, 06.*

MR. MORRIS
> *Thanks. Please write those numbers for the date.*
> Skipping a beat before:
> *Dyllon, what were those three numbers?*

DYLLON
> Having learned Mr. Morris expected everyone to pay attention to what students said:
> *10, 4, 06.*

MR. MORRIS
> With a wink in his direction:
> *Thank you. The next line down is for you to write the name of the student you were talking to. So, stop and think for a moment. Which student in our room are you most likely to talk to when you shouldn't be talking?*

This one is going to cause a bit of commotion as they ponder the possibilities. Just remain calm and quiet.

MR. MORRIS
> *Write that person's name on the line. Don't worry about spelling.*
> A brief pause.
> *Now, take a look at the list of things you should have been doing instead of talking. And, by the way, the bottom one is for a situation that is not covered by the other four. For example, maybe you were talking during an assembly. Anyway, put a check mark in front of the one that causes you the biggest problem. Do you talk to a neighbor during a lesson? Do you talk instead of working on your assignment? Do you talk during group work? Do you talk instead of reading silently?*

Give them some time on this one. Of all the funny things, they're going to want to talk this over with their neighbors. Enjoy the irony.

MR. MORRIS
> Wrapping up the demo:
> *And that's it. I'd like these back now, please.*
> Pausing as they are being collected.
> *Any questions?*

Yeah, Mr. Morris. Could you do a sample? Sure, I can. Thanks for asking.

Giving Out Yellow Slips

You first need to xerox a bunch of yellow slips. (The blackline master is on the last page of this chapter.) Cut the copies into fourths. Then, place a stack of them on your desk and maybe a stack of them near your class library. Here a stack, there a stack. Having them conveniently located will make distribution a bit easier.

When you see two or more students engaged in social talk, walk over to them, and give each one a yellow slip.

> MR. MORRIS
> Strong but soft:
>> *You guys are talking instead of reading independently. Not okay. Please fill out these yellow slips.*

You can almost predict one of the students will switch to classroom-lawyer mode.

> FUTURE LAWYER
> In a smooth attempt to defend the accusation:
>> *We were just talking about what we're reading.*

> MR. MORRIS
> Calmly:
>> *We agreed that during independent reading time, there was to be no talking of any kind. Fill out the form, please.*

> FUTURE LAWYER
> Going for an appeal:
>> *But I was only telling them to stop talking.*

> MR. MORRIS
> Not to be denied:
>> *You have a choice. You can fill it out now or you can fill it out at recess.*

And that usually does it. After filling them out, they'd hand me the slips. Notice, though, how I was able to avoid a no-win debate by choosing to use yellow slips during a time when there was no excuse for talking.[†] Test-taking time would be another good time to try out yellow slips. *Reality check:* Can you think of two students who would *not* try to explain away their social talking as nothing more than a discussion of the project on which they were both working? I can't.

Later on, when you've had a chance to refine your technique, you could expand it to other, more subjective situations that occur during the day.

Consequences

power
love
fun
freedom
safety

I wouldn't be in any rush to assign consequences for how many yellow slips students receive. Just use the first week to assess how many, overall, you're handing out. Maybe at

---

† The phrase I used was, "Not one word to one person." It was kinda hard to weasel out of that one.

the end of the week you could call aside the students who have decidedly more yellow slips than the other students.

MR. MORRIS
Speaking privately to five students:
You guys have many more yellow slips than the other students.
A hand held up to cut off any attempt at debate:
I'm not sure what we should do about it. I am certain, though, that it can't continue. Trust me when I say that social talking is not okay. If you need to be punished so that you realize I'm serious, I can punish you all.
Pausing to let that thought sink in:
I'd rather not punish anyone. I'd rather you all showed a bit more self-control. Speaking of which, what could you do the next time your neighbor starts a conversation during, say, independent reading time?

STUDENT 1
You could ask them to stop talking.

MR. MORRIS
You could, but then you'd be talking.

STUDENT 2
You could use the "I am ignoring you" sign.†

MR. MORRIS
Nodding his head in agreement:
That's a great idea. Why don't you try that the next time someone wants to talk to you at the wrong time. Any thoughts you'd like to share?

Our invented sign for, "I am ignoring you."

There won't be.

MR. MORRIS
Alrighty then. Back on task, eh?

Lookin' for the Good

Since you spoke with the students with the biggest collections of yellow slips, you should also gather up those students who didn't receive any.

MR. MORRIS
All smiles:
Fabulous. Not a yellow slip in the whole group. I'd like each of you to get a yellow slip and write a note on the back to your parents telling them you did not receive any yellow slips this week. When you're done, bring it to me, and I'll autograph it.

---

†   The use of this sign is described in the book *Tools & Toys*.

Beyond the First Week

Now that you've had a chance to run a trial period, you and your class can begin a discussion about what to do when someone gets 5, 10, or 15 yellow slips.

Whatever you and your students decide, you should probably set a level at which the consequence is to meet with the student and his parents. This isn't as grim as it sounds since you'll have a focus for these meetings.

> Mr. Morris
>> After welcoming comments have been made and everyone is seated comfortably:
>>> *As you probably know already, Calvin has received a number of yellow slips for social talking. Talking about a lesson or an activity is one thing. Social talking, though, is a concern, especially when we see how it is affecting his learning.*

I would then spread out the yellow slips so that his parents could see them all. The striking thing about the display was that, on 12 of the yellow slips, Calvin had checked the line in front of "working on my assignment."

Fig. 7-2
This is the truly powerful portion of the yellow slip. It's where Calvin indicated what he should have been doing instead of talking.

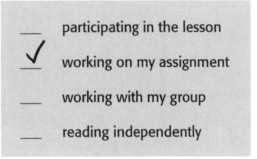

And in a very fundamental sense, this is why a yellow slip works so well: it's what I call a *behavior-specific* intervention. The majority of discipline programs we've seen over the years have been *consequence-specific*, i.e., we were taught to keep track of how many times rules were broken but we weren't keeping track of which rules were being broken.

Let's say that you're using the colored-cards-in-the-pocket-chart as your discipline plan. Everyone starts the day with the red-colored square showing on the chart. Red, the hue of love, is the best color you can have. Calvin, though, breaks one of the class rules. As a consequence, his red square is removed from his pocket on the chart which exposes his orange card. By the end of the day, Calvin has burned through orange, yellow, and green. His pocket is currently showing blue, the next-to-the-last color.

Here's my question: Would you be able to tell me, at the end of the day, what misbehavior got him down to blue?[†] I'm afraid the answer would be: "Nope. Not a clue."

Conclusion: Before we can expect a child to change his negative behavior, it's imperative that we are aware of the specific behavior that needs to be changed.

---

†   And what about other students who ended up on blue? How'd they get there?

Focus on the Behavioral Need

The beauty of using behavior-specific interventions is the ability to spotlight the actual behavior that is currently blocking the child's path to success. As you just saw on the previous page, the yellow slips actually documented the fact that Calvin had been talking socially when he should have been working on his assignment. The social talk is a roadblock: a fact that will be crystal clear to you, the student, and the parents. Without passing judgement or assigning blame, you merely share the reality of the present situation. Then, when everyone understands what's going on, the focus shifts to helping him overcome his propensity to talk instead of working on an assignment.

Beyond Yellow Slips

You could, of course, expand the basic concept so that it deals with more than one behavior. Shown below is a sample of a form I used in my room for years. Similar to its cousin, the yellow slip, the "pink slip" is a behavior-specific intervention. But instead of addressing just one behavior, it covers ten of them: the ten standards from the section of our report card that dealt with citizenship, work skills, and study habits.

FIG. 7-3
This is a sample of a pink slip, which is just an expanded version of the yellow slip.

MAKING BETTER CHOICES

Student #

Name: _____   Date: ____ / ____ / ____

I didn't make a good choice today. I didn't obey one of our classroom rules. (You can see the rule I checked below.)

I'm going to make a better choice next time.

STAY ON TASK	DO NEAT, CAREFUL WORK
COMPLETE WORK ON TIME	CLASSROOM BEHAVIOR
WORK COOPERATIVELY	PLAYGROUND BEHAVIOR
FOLLOW DIRECTIONS	RESPECT RIGHTS OF OTHERS
LISTEN TO LEARN	PRACTICE SELF-DISCIPLINE

☐ Student comments on back.   ☐ Teacher comments on back.

Just a thought:

If these ten standards are so important that they are on our district's report card, shouldn't they also, by default, be the operating standards (the actual rules for student conduct) in every classroom in our district?

Getting Serious

Everything up to this point was written with the assumption that you do not have that many students who actually engage in social talk. Or, if you decide to try the pink slip idea, it's because you don't have that many students not abiding by your ten standards. Either way, the slips work best when you have a relatively compliant class.

However, when you're getting overwhelmed by the sheer number of students who don't seem to care about following the rules—which was how I felt way back on page 134—it's going to take a serious effort to get things under control. In other words, when the misbehaviors begin to feel like misdemeanors, you know it's time to step it up a notch.

Behavior CODES

Okay. Twelve pages later and we're finally back to the actual strategy the chapter was named for. Please forgive the digression. I just felt it was important to point out that, when it comes to discipline, you can sometimes get by with less.

Unfortunately, though, by the second week of that new school year, I knew that less was not going to be enough. That is, passing out a thousand slips of paper—either yellow or pink—just wasn't going to cut it with this new group. I needed a discipline tool that could be set to "crowd control." Hence, the ADOPT technique.

You're about to discover that ADOPT will be easy for you to use, enable you to monitor your entire class, and be specific enough that you will have the ability to document and report on individual behavior.

Getting Started

Seating Chart
The first order of business is to create a seating chart.[†]

Amanda 02	Anthony 03	Calvin 06		Brie 05	Ben 04	Jesse 11
Nicole 15						Jessica 12

Daniel 07					Alyssa 01
Alejandro 13	Morgan 14	Dyllon 08	Jaime 09	Jeremy 10	Nikki 16
Valerie 19					Tim 18
Vincent 20					Shane 17

FIG. 7-4
Using a seating chart to record misbehavior, which I'm going to show you how to do, is better than a list of names. With the seating chart, where you look in the room is where you mark on the chart.

Myth Busters:

Don't be fooled into thinking this strategy only works with a small class.

I used ADOPT quite well with a class of 36 fifth graders.

---

† I made the one you see above with the grade-keeping program I used called *Easy Grade Pro.* (Check page 157 for info on this fabulous piece of software.) If you don't use a grade-keeping program or some other teacher utility program that will produce a seating chart, just make one on paper. It doesn't have to be pretty, merely accurate.

Put Copies of the Seating Chart on a Clipboard

After creating the chart, make five copies. Label them "Monday" through "Friday." Place the labeled chart on a clipboard. (I actually used a mini-clipboard. This type of clipboard, shown below, can be purchased at Staples or Office Depot and is a bit easier to use than the standard-sized model. *Note:* You'll need to xerox the copies with a 70% reduction in order to produce charts that will fit. Otherwise, use a normal clipboard. Your call.)

FIG. 7-5
It's kind of hard to see but there's a Pencil Caddy holding the pencil to the clipboard. It's one of my inventions that helped to make things manageable in my classroom.

Secondary Teachers:

Five separate seating charts for each of your classes might not be such a hot idea. It would probably make more sense to use a single grade sheet with five wide columns, one column for each day of the week.

You can find one on the New Management website by clicking on the Download Files link at the top of the main page.

Deciding on CODES

Part of what makes the whole thing work so well is that it's easy to use. This is primarily a result of how effortless it will be to document a student's misbehavior. Instead of handing out a yellow slip for social talking, for example, you merely write a letter code of your choosing in the student's seating box. There's no need for the student to fill out the form and then return it to you. Who's got time for that in the midst of a riot? The code will be enough.

Another part of its effectiveness is that you can use any code you wish. Here, again, are the codes I came up with and what they stood for.

A = not paying **A**ttention

D = not following **D**irections

O = not staying **O**n task

P = **P**laying around (Self-Control on the progress report)

T = not completing assignments on **T**ime

Since suggestions were already provided regarding how to deal with social talking, you might want to start with a one-letter code (T for talking) and focus on just that. Writing a dozen T's in seating boxes would be much easier than passing out twelve yellow slips. Also, by starting with just one code and one behavior, you'll be making your initial attempt to use ADOPT a more manageable one, which also means that you'll be more likely to stay the course.

For the Type-A overachievers out there who want to cover all of the bases, you could adjust the original ADOPT codes to incorporate social talking. Kind of like this:

A = not paying **A**ttention

D = not following **D**irections

O = not staying **O**n task

P = **P**unctuality (Assignments in on time.)

T = social **T**alking

The point I'm trying to make is this: The codes can be whatever you think they should be *and* can be changed if you need to change any of them.

Rethinking ADOPT

Speaking of change, the time has come to discontinue the use of the original ADOPT acronym and change it to something else. As it turns out, the use of the word *adopt* in conjunction with a program for documenting negative behavior was found to be offensive to a number of adoptive parents.

This was brought to my attention in March, 2010. An email I received alerted me about a comment that had been posted in the Yahoo adoptive community chatroom.

> *"Have any of you encountered a classroom management program called ADOPT? I was shocked when my 11-year-old adopted son came home from school to tell me that he had been "adopted" by his teacher. Evidently this means that his behavior in class that day was not good and he needed to be punished (or at least "monitored"). I emailed the teacher who told me that they were using a new class management program by Rick Morris called ADOPT (an acronym for: not paying Attention, not following Directions, being Off-task, Playing around, not turning in assignments on Time). Am I overreacting to this?"*

I responded immediately with the following post on my own website:

7

No. She's not over-reacting. She's merely expressing her concerns regarding the welfare of her son. In the thirty-one years I taught school, I was always most appreciative of the parents who brought these kinds of issues to my attention so that I could do something about them. After all, we both shared the same goal: helping children to achieve and succeed at the highest level.

And, true to form, I'm going to do something about this one.

Starting today, ADOPT will be removed as the title of the program and replaced with something less offensive. And that's an easy thing to do because the title of the discipline program I created is actually incidental and has nothing to do with adoption. It was just a clever—or so I thought—acronym to describe the five behaviors I was struggling to deal with one year.

So I'm going to rethink the acronym and come up with something harmless. Maybe we should have a contest and see who comes up with the best suggestion.

Off the top of my head, I'm thinking TODAY.

> *T = social Talking*
> *O = being Off-task*
> *D = not following Directions*
> *A = not paying Attention*
> *Y = Yelling (blurting, being too loud, etc.)*

But, then, that's just a quick thought. I'll come up with something.

To their credit, I received a number of emails and voice messages from the parents' group sharing their appreciation for my quick response and willingness to address the issue. I also received a couple of emails from teachers who sent in their suggestions.

LET'S NOT	**ADJUST**
Work missing or late	pay **A**ttention
Attention missing or lacking	follow **D**irections
Social talking	**J**ust stay on task
Time wasting (off-task behavior)	**U**nfinished assignments
Evading directions	**S**elf-control
OUR EDUCATION!	social **T**alking

But maybe instead of using TODAY or WASTE or ADJUST it would make more sense to forgo trying to make the behaviors we're dealing with fit into some kind of contrived title. As I mentioned in my response to the adoptive parents group, the use of ADOPT was incidental to its effectiveness. More than anything, it merely provided a convenient handle by which to identify the program. Shakespeare, speaking through Juliet, said, "What's in a name? That which we call an effective discipline program by any other name would work as well." Of course he was talking about roses as a metaphor for love, but you get the idea.

Bottom line: Don't let an acronym get in the way of an effective strategy.

My call, at least for the purposes of the next section that explains the actual strategy, is to use a workable substitute for the somewhat contentious ADOPT.

C = **C**ompletes assignments on time

O = stays **O**n task

D = follows **D**irections

E = **E**ngages during lessons

S = **S**ocial talking

Suggestion: Again, if you're not sure what codes to use, just start with one simple misbehavior and target that for a couple of weeks. You can always add codes or modify them as you gain experience and a deeper understanding of the needs of your students.

Documenting Misbehavior

Introduce CODES to Your Students

So we've got our clipboard and a week's worth of seating charts clipped to it. It's now time to introduce this new technique to the students.

Mr. Morris
  With clipboard in hand:
  I've got a new idea I'd like to try. It's called CODES, and I think it's going to help our classroom become a better place.

Other than the last week of school, it really doesn't matter when you bring in a new idea. Even if you've been using the colored-cards-in-the-pocket-chart thing for six months, you could easily incorporate CODES into your discipline program. For some reason, it seems as if adults have a harder time adapting to change than do students. So, don't worry about where you are in the school year or what you've already been doing. Just give it a shot and see how it goes. What have you got to lose?

MR. MORRIS
Showing everyone the clipboard and seating charts:
I've got a little clipboard with a seating chart on it. I'm going to use it to keep track of student behavior.
Pausing as students look around to figure out who the misfits are:
So, from now on, when I see that a student did not complete an assignment on time, or is not on task, or is not following directions, or is not engaged in a lesson, or is chit-chatting with a neighbor, I'm going to make a note on the seating chart. This will show me who needs extra help at being more responsible.

It actually doesn't matter what I said at this point in the game. My students were going to need to experience CODES before it began to make any sense to them. With that thought in mind, I kept the explanation short and sweet.

Using CODES During a Lesson

We're in the middle of a science lesson, and Calvin is furtively digging through his desk.

power
love
fun
freedom
safety

MR. MORRIS
Calmly, with clipboard in one hand and pencil in the other:
Calvin. The lesson is happening right now.[†] You need to stay with us.

I would write an **E**—not engaged in the lesson—in his seating box, pause while he complies, return the clipboard to my desk, and then proceed with the lesson.

Sounds easy enough, Rick. Couple of thoughts, though.

<u>What if Calvin were to offer a verbal defense?</u> I would gently cut off the dialogue.

CALVIN
But I was looking for my pencil.

MR. MORRIS
See me later. We'll talk about it. Right now, you need to pay attention to the lesson.

<u>What if the clipboard isn't within reach?</u> I would have someone get it for me.

MR. MORRIS
Looking over at the reading table, seeing the clipboard, and pointing at it:
Clipboard, please.

Whereby someone would get up and bring it to me. While I was waiting, which wasn't long, I didn't say a word. When I had it, I would write the letter and then proceed.

[†]   There were a number of phrases that didn't make the final cut for Chapter 3: The Top Ten Things I Say. "The lesson is happening right now," was one of them. It's a great way to refocus someone's wandering attention.

Using CODES During Independent Work

We're in the middle of our literacy block. I'm meeting with a small group at the reading table. The other students are engaged independently. I look across the room, though, and see four boys kickin' back instead of working on their vocabulary assignment.

MR. MORRIS
> To the small group:
> > *You guys keep reading together. I'll be right back.*
> Approaching the boys with clipboard in hand:
> > *Boys, what are you doing?*

SPOKESBOY
> *Working on vocabulary.*

MR. MORRIS
> *Correct. Problem is, you're not work-ing. You're actually off-task.*
> Marking an **O**—not staying on-task—in each of their seating boxes:
> > *Gentlemen, back on task, please.*

And with that, the point is made. Mr. Morris is going to be holding each student accountable for his behavior.

Making a Point With CODES

We're a minute away from morning recess. I cue up *Bill Nye, the Science Guy*, on my iPod and hit PLAY. My students hear the song and join me on the carpet.

MR. MORRIS
> With clipboard in hand:
> > *I'm going to read some names. If I read your name, I'd like you to stand. Anthony, Brie, Ben, Jessica, Alejandro, Morgan, and Vincent.*
> Pausing to make sure they are all standing.
> > *You guys do not have a single mark on the clipboard. Excellent. You may go to recess.*

And with that, the point is made. Mr. Morris is going to be holding each student ac-countable for his behavior. No more hiding out. No more verbal broadsides. Just a clear, calm focus. I would pause to allow those thoughts to sink in before I continued.

MR. MORRIS
> *Amanda, Nicole, Daniel, Valerie, Tim, and Shane.*
> I can almost guarantee they'd stand without being asked.
> > *Thanks for standing up. Each of you only have one mark on the clipboard. Not bad. Bye-bye.*
> Another pause.
> > *Alyssa, Nikki, Dyllon, Jesse, Jaime, and Jeremy. Thanks for standing. You have two marks each. You might want to think about your choices. You may go to recess.*

And now, sitting somewhat alone on the carpet, is our buddy, Calvin.

MR. MORRIS
  Showing him the chart:
    Here are your marks. Can you tell me what you need to work on?

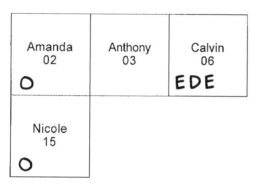

FIG. 7-6
Amanda and Nicole were not **O**n task. Calvin was not **E**ngaged during a lesson and not following **D**irections. Anthony is doing just fine.

CALVIN
  I need to work on paying attention.

Ah, the magic of using a behavior-specific tool. How clear it all becomes.

MR. MORRIS
  Nodding in agreement:
    Yes, the E stands for engagement. I'm glad you realize that. Anything I can do to help?

CALVIN
  No. I can do it. It's just hard sometimes.

MR. MORRIS
  I understand. It's just something to work on this year.
  Wanting to end on a somewhat positive note:
    *Did you notice you weren't the only one with marks? Look at Amanda's and Nicole's seating boxes. They were off task which is why you see the **O**. Just wanted you to know you're not the only one getting codes on the chart.*
  Standing up:
    Come on. Let's head outside for some recess. I could use a break. How about you?

CODES Will Get Better

As you were able to see in the three examples presented, the CODES program is easy to use. You just write a letter in a seating box. Before too long, all you'll need to do is *call* for your clipboard, and you'll see an improvement in their behavior. It's the whole actions backing up words thing that is the heart and soul of Core Principle #2.

With just a bit of practice and experience, you'll find yourself using the clipboard, and the information on the seating charts, in new ways. It won't happen overnight, but it will happen. Now, let's move on and create some progress reports for the parents to see.

Progress Reports

Before I show you the two different ways you can generate progress reports to send home with the students, let me suggest that you hold off on doing that right away. Since it's hard to predict how CODES is going to work in your room, I think it would be best for everyone involved if you were to engage in a "test run" for the first month. I can think of two advantages for trying CODES on a trial basis.

Teacher Advantage:

By using CODES in your class, but not sending home progress reports, you'll be allowing yourself an opportunity to try it on and see if you really like it. If, after a month or so, you find it's really meeting your needs, you can then add the progress report and take the strategy to a new level.

On the other hand, if you *had* sent home progress reports for a few weeks and *then* decided CODES was not a good fit, it might prove awkward to suddenly quit using it. I'm not saying you couldn't still bag the whole thing; but, I can almost guarantee you'd have parents asking, "Hey. What happened to those great progress reports you were sending home?"

Student Advantage:

The first month of using CODES is going to be an eye-opener for your students. I think it's only fair to allow them a bit of a honeymoon period before you start sending home the results for the folks to see. This will provide everyone with a chance to figure out how CODES works and what your standards are going to be. After that, it's open season.

Gathering the Results

Whether you decide to use the blackline master I've provided on the next page or the computer-generated progress reports I'll show you how to make in just a bit, you're going to need to process the seating charts and transfer the information to a grade sheet. This is not as difficult as it sounds. Let me show you.

Progress Reports Jan. 8-12		C	O	D	E	S
Alyssa	1	0	2	2	4	3
Amanda	2	2	1	3	2	0
Anthony	3	0	0	0	1	0
Ben	4	0	0	0	0	0
Brie	5	1	0	1	0	0
Calvin	6	1	2	5	5	3
Daniel	7	1	2	2	0	2

FIG. 7-7
By saving these weekly score sheets, you'll be able to maintain a record of your students' behavior.

1. Label a grade sheet with the codes.
2. Spread out the five seating charts so that you can see them all.
3. Start with the first student on your list and tally the results from the five charts.
4. Do this for each of your students.

Piece o' cake.

By the way: I did the score processing over the weekend because I sent home the results on the following Monday. I used to send them out on Friday, but it just didn't work well. For one, it was a hassle trying to prepare everything to be ready before Friday's dismissal time. For another, it was hard for my students to remember to return the reports after a long weekend. Probably the most important reason I switched to Mondays, though, was a psychological one. I wanted the reports to have a more immediate impact. It was better, I discovered, to hand out the previous week's results at the beginning of the new week. This really helped to get everyone refocused and thinking about our standards.

Secondary Teachers

To make this part of CODES manageable, you might want to think about sending home reports for just the students who did a great job and the students who really need some intervention. Don't worry about the group in the middle right now. You can get to them later on after you've had a chance to get the whole process dialed in.

Using a Blackline Master

Here's the blackline master I mentioned on the previous page. You are welcome to use it as-is or allow it to inspire you to create your own report.

BEHAVIOR PROGRESS REPORT

For the week of: _____

Student name: _____   Date: _____

Listed below are the total reminders you were given at school last week. Please go over this report with your parents and have one of them sign it. Return it to class tomorrow.

	NUMBER OF REMINDERS
Completes Assignments	
Stays On Task	
Follows Directions	
Engages During Lessons	
Social Talk	

_____
Parent signature

Comments:

Make Copies

1. Fill in the "Week of:" information on two bulletins.
2. Lay these on the xerox machine.
3. Make your copies and then cut them in half.

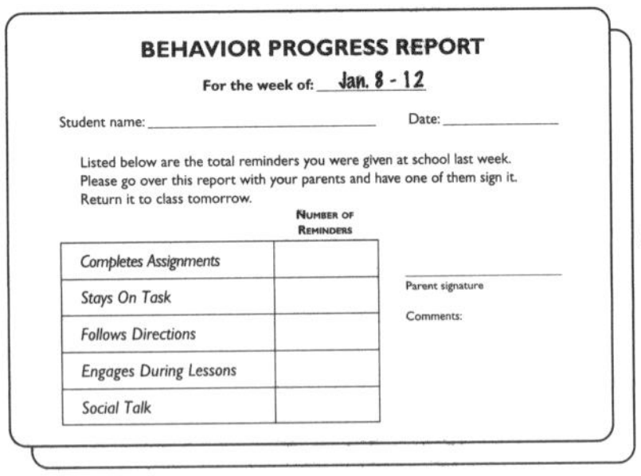

BEHAVIOR PROGRESS REPORT
For the week of: Jan. 8 - 12
Student name: _____ Date: _____
Listed below are the total reminders you were given at school last week. Please go over this report with your parents and have one of them sign it. Return it to class tomorrow.

	NUMBER OF REMINDERS
Completes Assignments	
Stays On Task	
Follows Directions	
Engages During Lessons	
Social Talk	

Parent signature
Comments:

BEHAVIOR PROGRESS REPORT
For the week of: Jan. 8 - 12
Student name: _____ Date: _____
Listed below are the total reminders you were given at school last week. Please go over this report with your parents and have one of them sign it. Return it to class tomorrow.

	NUMBER OF REMINDERS
Completes Assignments	
Stays On Task	
Follows Directions	
Engages During Lessons	
Social Talk	

Parent signature
Comments:

BEHAVIOR PROGRESS REPORT
For the week of: Jan. 8 - 12
Student name: _____ Date: _____
Listed below are the total reminders you were given at school last week. Please go over this report with your parents and have one of them sign it. Return it to class tomorrow.

	NUMBER OF REMINDERS
Completes Assignments	
Stays On Task	
Follows Directions	
Engages During Lessons	
Social Talk	

Parent signature
Comments:

FIG. 7-8
I took two blank reports and created the master copy I'd use to xerox the ones for the students.

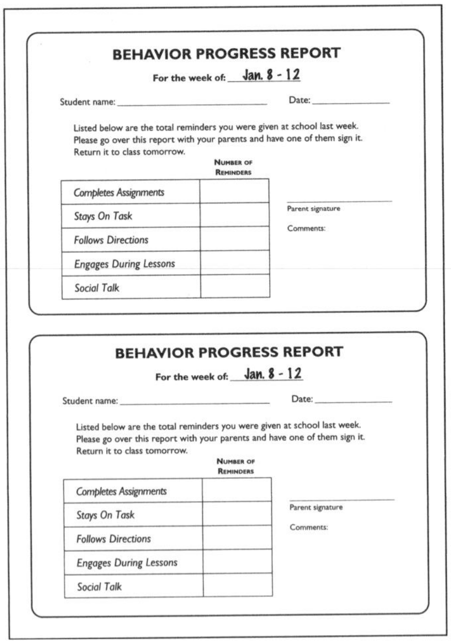

Pass Them Out

First thing Monday morning, I passed out copies of the progress report and had them fill in the name and date info.

MR. MORRIS

I'll be meeting with each of you during independent reading time to fill in your scores. If you have time, write your parents a note on the back of the report and tell them how you think you did last week. I'm guessing they would really like that.
Holding up the clipboard with the new seating charts on it:
By the way, there is not a single mark on today's seating chart. See what you can do to keep your little box spotless.

Meet With Students

As they worked independently, I called over students two or three at a time. Only one of them sat at the reading table with me. The others knew to give us some privacy. I then transferred the scores from the grade sheet to the child's progress report. I looked for good scores—which were the low ones—and marked them with a highlighter. It only took about thirty seconds per student.[†]

Send Them Home

At the end of the day, I reminded everyone about not only taking home the progress report but also bringing it back the next day. I'd then collect them on Tuesday—it took a couple of days for some—checked them over for parent comments, and then tossed 'em. You could always display the best ones if you wanted to. That could be kind of fun.

[†]   You might be thinking that it would be better to have the progress reports all prepared and filled out ahead of time. You are certainly welcome to do that if you wish. I like being able to see the child as I write the "reminder totals" in the five boxes. It gives me a chance to connect with them and makes things a bit more personal.

Computer Created Progress Reports

Although the progress reports you can make using the blackline master work great, some teachers have found they like the benefits of a computer-generated report. Using a computer to record the scores will provide you with an easy-to-access cumulative record. That's a bonus. The other benefit is how much easier it is to produce a replacement copy of a student's progress report because he "lost it" on the way home.

As I mentioned on page 146, I prefer Easy Grade Pro†. Like most software of this type, it enabled me to create both the seating chart and the progress reports I sent home.

Entering Their Scores

In order to produce an actual grade, Easy Grade Pro needed a possible score. Therefore, I had to assign a point value to each day. Since Monday, Tuesday, Thursday, and Friday were all full days, I assigned 3 points for each day. Wednesday was a minimum day so it was given 2 points. This produced a total possible score of 14 points for each category. Consequently, the score I entered for each student was calculated by subtracting the number of reminders from 14. (It's easier than it sounds.)

Points for the week for each of the five categories.

Mon. = 3
Tue. = 3
Wed. = 2
Thur. = 3
Fri. = 3

Total = 14

In the example shown below, Alyssa ended up with 12 points for Stays **O**n Task. During the week I had written an **O** in her seating box on two different occasions and, as we already know, 14 – 2 = 12. Therefore, I entered a 12 in that space.

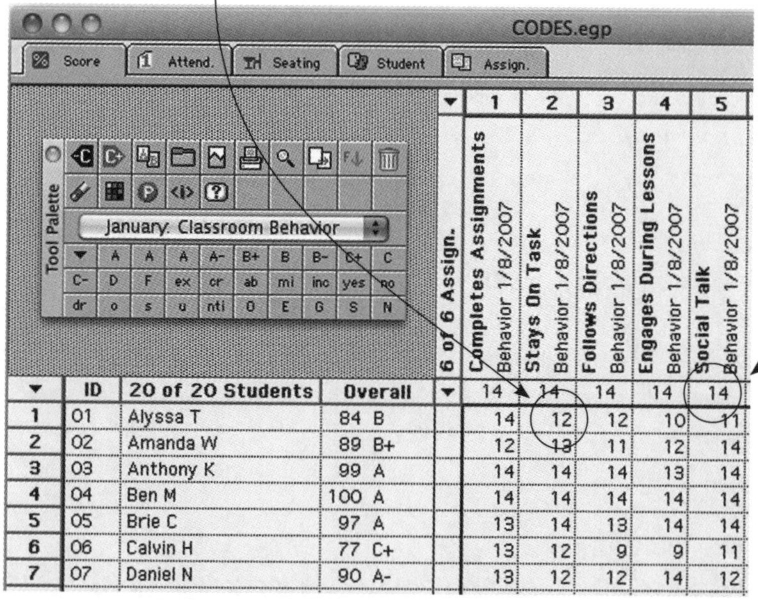

ID	20 of 20 Students	Overall	1 Completes Assignments Behavior 1/8/2007	2 Stays On Task Behavior 1/8/2007	3 Follows Directions Behavior 1/8/2007	4 Engages During Lessons Behavior 1/8/2007	5 Social Talk Behavior 1/8/2007
			14	14	14	14	14
01	Alyssa T	84 B	14	12	12	10	11
02	Amanda W	89 B+	12	13	11	12	14
03	Anthony K	99 A	14	14	14	13	14
04	Ben M	100 A	14	14	14	14	14
05	Brie C	97 A	13	14	13	14	14
06	Calvin H	77 C+	13	12	9	9	11
07	Daniel N	90 A-	13	12	12	14	12

FIG. 7-9 If you would like a copy of the grade-book I made for CODES, just send me an email.

Bonus: By assigning a point value to each day, you'll be able to maintain grading consistency during a shortened week. If, for example, Monday had been a holiday, the possible score for that week would be 11.

† I've tried a half dozen grade-keeping programs and have found *Easy Grade Pro* to be, by far, the best of the lot. It's not only easy to use, it also allows for a great deal of personalizing. Made for both PC and Mac platforms, you can find out more about this award-winning program on their website. The URL is: [http://www.easygradepro.com]. They even have a demo version that you can download and try.

Printing Progress Reports

After entering all of the scores, I then composed a note to go above the grade box and a note to go below it. It was fun to highlight students who had done especially well. Also, making the reports more personal helped to make them more meaningful.

STUDENT PROGRESS REPORT
Monday, January 15, 2007
JANUARY: CLASSROOM BEHAVIOR

Calvin H   Mr. Morris
Overall Grade: 77%   C+   Room 12

Here are your behavior grades for last week.

Congratulations to Ben, Lindsey, Nicole, Ryan, and Wesley who made the 3 R Club last week. (Their overall grades were 100%!)

January Assignments

#	Date	Category	Assignment	Score	Grade
1	1/8	Behavior	Completes Assignments	13/14	93% A-
2	1/8	Behavior	Stays On Task	12/14	86% B
3	1/8	Behavior	Follows Directions	9/14	64% D
4	1/8	Behavior	Engages During Lessons	9/14	64% D
5	1/8	Behavior	Social Talk	11/14	79% C+

Go over your grades with your parents, have one of them sign the report, and return it to class on Tuesday.

Thanks,
Mr. Morris

FIG. 7-10
There's nothing quite like an official-looking document to send a strong message.

I then printed the copies, handed them out, and had a word with a couple of students.

MR. MORRIS
Sitting with Calvin and his progress report:
So. What do you think?

CALVIN
Trying to make the best of it:
I need to work on paying attention to lessons and following directions.

MR. MORRIS
I agree. You might want to start by making good choices today. Any good stuff going on with your report?

CALVIN
Perking up a bit:
Yeah! I did a good job on turning in work. And pretty good at staying on task, too.

Usually, the negative students only hear the negative message. How sweet it is to share the good news as well. That's more than a great motivator; it's a relationship builder.

Using a Grade Sheet

After producing the progress reports, I printed out a grade sheet showing all of the scores. (I usually placed it on the clipboard underneath the new week's seating charts so that it was easy to get to.) I liked to use it to reward or recognize students for the good choices they had made the previous week. It was just another way to show my appreciation.

MR. MORRIS
> Reading from the grade sheet:
> *"The following students stayed on task all last week and may line up first for lunch.*
> Pausing before continuing:
> *Anthony, Ben, Brie, Dyllon..."*

FIG. 7-11
Using the scores from last week's behavior to improve this week's behavior is easy to do when you have the grade sheet on your clipboard.

	ID	20 of 20 Students	Overall	5 of 5 Assign.	Completes Assignments Behavior 1/8/2007	Stays On Task Behavior 1/8/2007	Follows Directions Behavior 1/8/2007	Engages During Lessons Behavior 1/8/2007	Social Talk Behavior 1/8/2007
					14	14	14	14	14
1	01	Alyssa T	84 B		14	12	12	10	11
2	02	Amanda W	89 B+		12	13	11	12	14
3	03	Anthony K	99 A		14	14	14	13	14
4	04	Ben M	100 A		14	14	14	14	14
5	05	Brie C	97 A		13	14	13	14	14
6	06	Calvin H	77 C+		13	12	9	9	11
7	07	Daniel N	90 A-		13	12	12	14	12
8	08	Dyllon I	94 A-		14	14	12	13	13

A Few Reminders

Other than the variations you'll come up with yourself, you now have a general idea of how it all works. We'll now close the chapter with a short list of reminders.

1. More action; less talk.

2. Make a fresh start. Show your students the blank seating chart at the beginning of every day. Encourage them to make good choices.

3. Keep yourself calm when you're in tough situations. Set the example.

4. Look for the good. Focus on the positive.

5. Read MacKenzie's book, *Setting Limits in the Classroom.*

Most importantly, remember that it's all about the safe and caring relationships you are trying to develop with your students.

A Reminder About Staying On Task

Name/#: _____   Date: ___/___/___

I was talking to _____   instead of:

___ participating in the lesson

___ working on my assignment

___ working with my group

___ reading independently

___

☐ student comments on back   ☐ teacher comments on back

A Reminder About Staying On Task

Name/#: _____   Date: ___/___/___

I was talking to _____   instead of:

___ participating in the lesson

___ working on my assignment

___ working with my group

___ reading independently

___

☐ student comments on back   ☐ teacher comments on back

A Reminder About Staying On Task

Name/#: _____   Date: ___/___/___

I was talking to _____   instead of:

___ participating in the lesson

___ working on my assignment

___ working with my group

___ reading independently

___

☐ student comments on back   ☐ teacher comments on back

A Reminder About Staying On Task

Name/#: _____   Date: ___/___/___

I was talking to _____   instead of:

___ participating in the lesson

___ working on my assignment

___ working with my group

___ reading independently

___

☐ student comments on back   ☐ teacher comments on back

Chapter Eight

Core Principles

Confessions of a Former Echoer

The Top Ten Things I Said

Using Music for
Student Independence

Sentence Strips
Cut-and-Paste Paragraphs

Homework Made Easier

Behavior CODES

Credit Cards

Sometimes, the best way to double your money
is to fold it in half and put it back in your pocket.

—Alfred E. Newman

Chapter 8
Credit Cards

◆ ◆

Goals for this chapter:

☑ Understand the benefits and drawbacks of traditional reward/recognition programs.

☑ Learn how the basic Credit Card program works.

☑ Realize that delayed gratification can enhance a student's development.

☑ Discover ways to help your students become goal-oriented.

◆ ◆

I'm going to end this book with something fun. One of those signature things I did over the years, Credit Cards was always a student favorite.

But, first, a little background.

power
love
fun
freedom
safety

Research, which can be used to support a multiplicity of theories, is rather one-sided in its assessment of reinforcement and the effect it has upon students. According to all of the major findings, positive reinforcement is, without question, the hands-down winner when it comes to developing the characteristics of independence, responsibility, and self-discipline.

If you were to compare two classes, one experiencing positive reinforcement (behavior modification, an Orwellian term at best) and the other experiencing negative reinforcement (aversive conditioning), you would find that the students from the positive class come out miles ahead in behavior, self-esteem, and, most importantly, achievement.

Does this mean, then, that you should drop your classroom rules and consequences in favor of a positive approach? No, not at all. Why settle for using just one form of discipline? The optimal learning environment takes advantage of both systems—clearly defined rules with consequences for non-compliance *and* recognition for exemplary behavior and achievement—to produce the desired results. By using both forms of reinforcement, your students will develop a well-rounded awareness of right and wrong in addition to the desire to follow the correct course when faced with multiple choices.

So, with research gently guiding us down the positive path, the only challenge educators face becomes the rather formidable task of coming up with a system for rewarding behavior and achievement which is simple, yet effective. Let's face it. Before any reward system can be effective for a group of students, it must first meet the criterion of simplicity for their teacher. Really now, who wants to spend a major portion of each day feeling like Randy the Reward King or Mrs. Stickerbook?

When I looked around as a new teacher to see what other teachers were doing to create a positive classroom atmosphere, I discovered there were three standard reward/recognition programs in use. All three of them were good in certain ways, but each one had its fundamental flaws which made using it somewhat problematic.

Class Cash

Fake money has been around for quite a long time. Part of its popularity stems from the fact that it mirrors the real world. Students like just about anything that simulates actual life, and cash is one of those things that makes the classroom seem larger than normal.

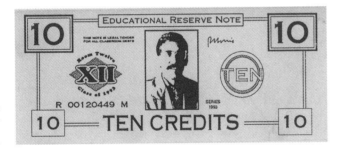

FIG. 8-1
There's nothing like cash to stimulate a little interest in what's going on in the room.

Another advantage to cash is its tangibility. Students can hold it in their hands. It's real. It's concrete. We're talkin' cold, hard cash. And because the students have the cash, they are the ones who control the purse strings.[†]

power
love
fun
freedom
safety

Just slap down a couple of Happy Bucks at the classroom mini-mart and pick up a new pencil, a treat, or a special privilege. That's a great feeling for a kid, especially one who may be living in a home where there's not much money for the extra things.

Relatively easy for the teacher to create, a token economy system can be a bit of hassle to maintain. Keeping the money organized so that it's manageable to pay students when you need to can get a bit tricky. It is definitely fun, though, to be King of the Realm and hand out some cash in recognition of the attitudes and behaviors you want to reinforce.

Sounds pretty good so far. What's the downside, Rick?

The downside to classroom money, and it's a big one, is the theft issue. The feelings of betrayal and distrust that result from the loss of their hard-earned cash can act as a deterrent to your attempts to get everyone to bond into some type of second family. Having the students write their names on their bills, which is the traditional teacher response to theft, is weak, at best. For one, what does it imply about the safety of your room? And, for another, do you really want to be printing money on a weekly basis?

---

†   Or don't control the purse strings, as the case may be. Some of them will spend it as soon as they get it. Others will save it to use later. These kinds of "real life" experiences can help to prepare them to be more successful adults.

Table Points

Another standard recognition system is the use of table points, or team points, in which predetermined groups of students—usually students who are sitting together—are given points for their behavior and achievement.

Students, for the most part, like team points. Even though there is nothing to hold in your hands the way you can with class cash, the evidence of how your team is doing is right there on the board for all to see.

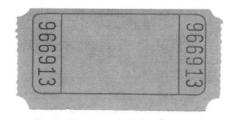

FIG. 8-2 Colored triangles of construction paper taped to the whiteboard create an easy-to-use location for keeping track of the points each team has earned.

TEACHER
Looking at tallies on the whiteboard:
The Yellow Team has eight points. Way to go, Yellows. You may choose the game we're going to play for P.E. today.

Similar to cash, table points are easy for the teacher to set-up. All you need is a bit of space on your whiteboard and a way to indicate, or label, each team's space. (I've found colored triangles of construction paper taped to the whiteboard to be perfect for this.)

As opposed to cash, team points are very easy for the teacher to use. All that's needed is a whiteboard marker. Either the teacher can record the points or, as I prefer, the students can make the little stick marks.

The big flaw with team points is that it's a team-based system. For the Yellow Team, life is good; the sun is shining; it's clear skies ahead. For the Green Team—the team residing just below the Yellow Team in Fig. 8-2 above—the sun is not shining quite so brightly. In fact, the Green Team's parade is getting rained on. And, in a breaking story, the weatherman is predicting the approach of a storm front because he can foresee that friction and frustration are going to boil over as the team tries to deal with its dysfunction.

power
love
fun
freedom
safety

Coupons

I loved coupons.† They were easy to use and fun for the students.

FIG. 8-3 You can find inexpensive coupons at Smart & Final.

More importantly, they reinforced Maslow's findings about the intermittent reward being the most effective type of reinforcement. Coupons, by their very nature, mirrored that. I could pass out all of the coupons I wished in an effort to recognize all of the behavior and achievement I

---

† Check the *Tools & Toys* book for a three-page dissertation on the joy of coupons.

deemed appropriate and important. Whether a student actually won something for the coupons he had received depended, of course, upon one of his coupons being pulled from the container in which they were deposited. And, boy, did they enjoy the suspense and drama of the draw and the announcement of the winning six-digit number. Yahtzee!

The big problem with coupons was also a part of their attractiveness: the randomness of the draw. I'd hate to think there was some kind of a Las Vegas point-spread on the reward part. I'd rather that it were a bit more predictable for the students and not quite so dependent on the luck of the draw.

> *Thought for the day:* Another little thing about coupons—and cash and team points, now that I think about it—is the immediacy of the pay-out. Your coupon was pulled? Here's your reward. You earned a couple of bucks? Go ahead and buy something. Your team has the most points right now? Your team may go to lunch right now.
>
> I don't know. Maybe it's just me, but I think lessons are being learned with any kind of reward system, and I want to make sure the lessons my students learn are the right ones. Wouldn't it be better for them if they had to wait a bit—that is, learned to develop the ability to defer immediate self-gratification—before they were able to cash in? Actually, it would.
>
> In the famous "marshmallow studies" conducted at Stanford University, four-year-olds were asked to stay in a room alone with a marshmallow and wait for a researcher to return. They were told that if they could wait until the researcher came back before eating the first one, they would be given an extra one. Ten years later, the researchers talked with the study participants. Their discovery? The kids who were able to resist the temptation to eat the marshmallow—an example of deferred gratification—outscored the ones who weren't able to wait by over 200 points on the SAT. Pretty amazing.

The Final Results

Having looked at the three traditional recognition systems out there and considered their good points and their weaknesses, we can now tabulate the results.

	CLASS CASH	TEAM POINTS	COUPONS
tangible, concrete, hold-it-in-your-hands	✓		✓
easy for the teacher to manage		✓	✓
easy for the students to redeem	✓	✓	✓
simulates the real world	✓		
focused on the individual	✓		✓
theft-proof		✓	
has a consistent, predictable value	✓		
helps students learn to defer gratification			

FIG. 8-4
You can see that all three systems have their pluses and minuses.

Class Cash, it seemed, had the most advantages and was closest to what I was looking for. But, the theft issue was a killer. If there was something similar to cash but without the fear of theft—not to mention the hassle of keeping the cash organized yet convenient to get my hands on when needed—I would be one happy boy.

So, back in 1981, after a little noodling, I came up with the Credit Card idea: a 5 X 8 index card kept by each student on which I would stamp little stars, or credits.

FIG. 8-5
Here we see Calvin's card and the eight credits he has earned so far.

Credit Cards

There were so many things to like about Credit Cards. For one, the whole thing was so easy to use. Easy for me; easy for them. For another, the card was a tangible, hold-it-in-your-hand kind of thing. A big bonus was safety. Students kept their Credit Cards at their desks *but* didn't have to worry about theft. That's because every card was identified with a name and a student number. Lastly, credits were earned for individual initiative, which I preferred, and the cash-in part, which required a bit of deferment, was a snap.

All-in-all, a winner.

What You Need
To get started, you only need two things: a rubber stamp and a packet of 5 x 8 plain index cards. That's it.

The star stamp is a self-inking model (#11309) made by Xstamper. It makes an impression of a small, red star. (The impression to the right shows the actual size.) You can find one at Staples or Office Depot for about seven bucks.

The index cards are used by the students. These cards are signed by the students and kept at their desks. And although this takes some practice to get down—every student has to figure out the best way to maintain his own card—they eventually get to the point whereby the card is handy but not a distraction. Just think of it as another opportunity for your students to exercise responsibility and self-control.

The Big Picture

To reward a student, a star, or *credit* as we called it, is stamped on his card. Whenever a student has earned fifteen credits—a completely arbitrary number which can be adjusted to fit your needs—he is entitled to some predetermined reward. In our room, the reward was lunch in the classroom with me. Since it usually took a couple of weeks for most students to earn 15 credits, I scheduled the first lunch a month after we began using credits.

Getting Started

I'm going to assume two things: 1) you have your stamp, and 2) the students each have a 5 x 8 index card identified with a name and a student number. Of course, as soon as you asked them to do that, they wanted to know why.

The Goal

Mr. Morris
    With credit stamp in hand:
        These cards are going to be called Credit Cards.
    Mumble, mumble, buzz, buzz:
        Your card is where I will stamp little stars which we're going to call "credits."
    Demonstrates by stamping his own card and showing the class:
        That's a credit. When you have earned 15 of them, which is going to take you a couple of weeks, you'll be having lunch in the classroom with me and anyone else who has earned 15 credits.
    Walking over to the big wall calendar and circling the last Friday of the month:
        Our first lunch is going to be held on Friday, the 28th. If you have earned 15 credits by then, you'll be invited to lunch. Here's what the invitation looks like.

Fig. 8-6 You may use this coupon if you wish or make your own. You can even dispense with the invitation since the Credit Cards can serve as their tickets to lunch .

The Reality of the Goal

If lunch in your classroom is not a practical reward for your hard workers, come up with something that they'll think is special. Maybe you could provide an after-lunch treat or have Domino's deliver a pizza at the end of the day. Whatever fits your needs. *Something to remember:* They really like being with you doing something special.

One suggestion I'll make about the reward is to limit the offer. Similar to the recommendation at the top of page 154 about trying the CODES program for a month before sending home a progress report, I think it might be helpful for you to try Credit Cards for just a month. This will give you an opportunity to try it on and see what you think. If you decide, after you've held your first lunch, that you like the whole thing, you could then try it for another month. What I'm getting at is there is no need to make a long-term commitment to using credits. Just take 'em for a run and see what happens.

Some teachers use Credit Cards for a month, do the lunch thing, and collect everyone's card. Then, after a month or two has passed, they bring out the cards, announce the date of the next lunch, and let their students experience credits a second time. One advantage to this variation is that the students who had only earned 8 or 9 credits the first time will already have a head start on earning credits for the new lunch. Consequently, they'll be more likely to reach 15 and be able to enjoy the reward.

As always, it's your call.

The Rules

MR. MORRIS

power
love
fun
freedom
safety

> *There are just two simple rules to follow. Rule Number 1: Your Credit Card is your responsibility. You can keep it in your desk or use it as a bookmark. It doesn't matter. What does matter is that you hang on to it. When you lose your card, then you lose the credits that were on the card. I won't replace them. So, please, take care of your card.*

The Reality of the First Rule

They're going to lose their cards. Trust me on this one. It happened every year to even the most responsible of students. To make the replacement process easy, I learned to have a stack of blank index cards on hand. What I also learned was not to stamp the new card with the credits that had been earned on the first card. Losing your credits because you lost your card—a *natural consequence*—was a life lesson all by itself.

There will be times, though, when a student finds his original card that he thought had been lost. In this situation, have him choose the card he's going to keep using. Take the other card, fold it in half, and staple it shut. This will prevent him from having credits stamped on two different cards. As I told my students, "Eight credits on one card and seven credits on another card ain't fifteen. It's *eight* and *seven*. You must have fifteen credits on one card in order to purchase a ticket to lunch."

Mr. Morris
Continuing where he left off before he was interrupted by an aside about The Reality
of the First Rule:

*Rule Number 2: Please don't ask me for a credit. I want to be able to give out credits
without being hounded about it. Besides, you all have a month to earn 15. So, relax,
and let me take care of you.*

Big smile for the finale:

*One last thing. It's okay to remind me about paying you a credit. Let's say that I
had told the Blue Team that I would pay each of them a credit for their outstanding
behavior at this morning's assembly but I hadn't paid them yet. I would want one of
them to remind me about it. But, other than a reminder, please don't ask for credits.*

The Reality of the Second Rule

Students will test your limits about not asking for credits. I heard all of the variations
over the years and can tell you that they fall into two basic categories.

The first category is comprised of students who offer to take care of some task for a
credit.

Limit-Testing Student
Will you give me a credit if I clean up our library?

Mr. Morris
With a calm but serious look:

*If you'd like to clean up the library on your own, that would be great. Just don't expect
to be paid for it. Thanks.*

The second category, which is a little more difficult to handle at first, occurs when a student complains about the teacher not being fair about paying credits.

Student
Trying to extort a credit with an outburst:

How come she got a credit? I was doing that, too!

The experience I gained from using Credit Cards for so long enabled me to take this kind
of complaint and turn it into a lesson. As opposed to repeating the same message to the
ten different students who might try the same tactic, I learned that it was better to bring
up this issue with the entire class. It was one of those "relationship moments."

Mr. Morris
Having gathered everyone on the carpet:

*Let's talk about credits for a minute. I'm glad you like your Credit Cards. Every class
I've ever taught has loved their Credit Cards. Credits are here to stay. However, if you
are consumed with getting credits, you are in for some disappointment because I won't*

pay you for every good thing you do in here. Scientists have found out that it's not good for you.[†] So, don't waste any class time thinking, 'How can I get a credit?' You need to relax and not worry about it. You can't force credits onto your card. In fact, it's when you let go of credits that they're more likely to come to you.

Pausing for that to sink in before:

If you consistently take care of yourself in this room, you'll consistently receive credits. It just won't happen every time. Okay, back on task, please.

Earning Credits

So that the students in that second category—the ones who were concerned about how they were going to get their 15 credits—didn't become a thorn in the side of my class, I eventually published a list of ways in which a student could earn a credit without having to ask for one. By turning their attention to the "goal sheet," I was able to redirect their energy about earning credits instead of suppressing it.

Credits Earned by Students

Here are just a few of the many goals you could set for your students. This list can be especially helpful when a student is at 13 credits and the lunch day is getting closer.

★ <u>Turning in all four homework assignments:</u> For the child who usually turns in two or three of the four assignments, the credit being offered might be the incentive he needs to complete all four homework assignments. You never know.

★ <u>Perfect score on a quiz or test:</u> It's fun to pass back a test and pass out some credits. If no one has a perfect score, pay the students with the top score.

> *Word to the wise:* When you stamp the card, stamp the test. The red star on the test will remind you later that the student has already been paid.

★ <u>Classroom or school-wide competitions:</u> I got away from the Old School award philosophy in which there was a first-, second-, and third-place winner. Too many kids missed out. And the only truly happy one was the student who received the first-place award anyway. So, in lieu of that style, I presented awards to many students. One time, after an essay-writing contest, I gave out Certificates of Merit to ten students. In addition to their printed certificates, I also paid each one of them a credit.

---

† We know this is Maslow talking; they won't. But, whenever it's appropriate, I liked to share research—especially educational research—with my students.

★ Perfect attendance for a week: Why not institute a "Friday Payday" and pay a credit to every student who was not absent during the week? You could even have a student run it for you. First thing Friday morning you could collect the cards from the perfect attenders and give them to your student helper for stamping. It only stands to reason that paying a credit for attendance would lend a bit of credence to the slogan "Miss school, miss out."

power
love
fun
freedom
safety

★ Hat Trick, or scoring 3 pluses on your Center Stage card: On page 119, I talked about using a set of 3 x 5 index cards—with a student name on each card—in order to randomly call upon students to read a spelling sentence to the class. I mentioned, at the time, that index cards are great because you can record a plus, a check, or a minus based upon the student's performance. As I put the third plus on a student's card, I called out, "Hat Trick!" The student knew to bring me his card for a credit. Paying for every three pluses improved their oral language skills, fed their need for fun, and helped them develop the ability to delay gratification. Not bad.

power
love
fun
freedom
safety

★ Having a classroom job:† I didn't have students rotate through jobs with one student being ball monitor one week and someone else doing it next week. My feeling was that, if you want to be ball monitor and you're good at it, you should be able to keep your job. When you got bored with it or your job performance began to slip, then we found a replacement worker. *Minimum wage:* 1 credit per week.

> *Learn from my mistake:* One credit per week may not seem like much. Actually, it's not. However, I learned a valuable lesson my first year of using Credit Cards. We had been using credits for a number of weeks, and I wanted to rekindle their initial enthusiasm. The mistake I made was to pay two credits for certain things. Well, once I started to do that, they were no longer happy to receive just one. So, the lesson was, and still is: Only pay one credit at a time. It might be one for your top score on the math test *and* another one for loaning your neighbor a pencil without being asked, but it will always be just one.

As you can imagine, there are a boatload of goals you could set for your students to attain. And even though you might start with just two goals on your list, the message it sends will be loud and clear: Stop looking to me for a credit. Look to yourself instead.

Credits Given at the Teacher's Discretion

An advantage to the list of ways in which a student was guaranteed to earn a credit was the freedom I gained to pay credits as I saw fit. Having the posted goals was going to counter-balanced any bias that occurred when I passed out credits at my discretion. Bias, unintentional though it may be, happens, and it's important to keep it under control. With that in mind, let's discuss the many ways you could pay credits based upon nothing more than your desire to stimulate your students to be the best they can be.

---

† Check out Workers Ahead on the New Management website for my thoughts regarding classrooms jobs.

★ <u>Student of the Day:</u> The *Tools & Toys* book talks about giving out an award at the end of each day to a student in recognition of something noteworthy. Adding a credit to the presentation seems like a logical extension.

★ <u>Being a role model:</u> I always strove to encourage student initiative. It was one of the main things for which I paid credits. So, whenever I saw one of my students engaged in behavior which I wanted others to follow, I handed out a credit along with my appreciation.

MR. MORRIS
    Beckoning a student to his desk as he grabbed his credit stamp:
    Thanks for letting Nikki share your science book. That was a thoughtful thing to do, young man. Card, please.

Oh, did they like to hear me say those two words.

★ <u>Problem solving:</u> It was surprising how many times a student came up with some clever solution to a problem we were facing. Turned out all he needed was someone willing to listen to his suggestion with an open mind.

MR. MORRIS
    With sincere appreciation:
    Wow. Wouldn't have thought of that. Very nice idea. Card, please.

★ <u>Helping other students:</u> Without having to make a big deal about it—do a loud broadcast of your pleasure to the entire class—see if you can quietly pay a credit to students who, on their own initiative, engage in tutoring other students.

Extension: I'd pull two students aside just before recess and arrange a deal.

MR. MORRIS
    Speaking privately to Marisa with Quinn listening in:
    Quinn wants to study her vocabulary during recess because we're having a short quiz as soon as we come back in. She was looking for a tutor, and I thought you might be willing to help her.

MARISA
    Sure, Mr. Morris.

MR. MORRIS
    Great. Thanks for wanting to help. Tell you what, I'll pay you each a credit if Quinn gets a perfect score.

power
love
fun
freedom
safety

Granted, Marisa would have been happy to help Quinn without any compensation. Slipping them each a credit just added to my expression of thanks.

★ <u>Buying used paperback books from your students:</u> This proved to be a very effective way to build our classroom library without having to spend a dime. However, when I was paying credits for something the students brought in, I learned to put a cap on how much they could earn.

Mr. Morris
    Announcing to his students at the morning staff meeting:[†]
        If you have any paperback books at home in good condition that you think would
        make a nice addition to our library, I'd like to buy them from you for a credit each.
    Students quickly realizing the possibilities of a windfall before Mr. Morris adds:
        The most I'll pay is 5 credits. So, if you bring 10 books, I'll select 5 of them.

Do that a couple times during the school year—especially a month after a Scholastic book order has been delivered to your students—and your library will be overflowing with books.

★ <u>Rentals</u> Since my students liked to work on the grassy area outside our classroom, we made the area a little cosier by laying out old bedspreads and blankets. I "rented" the blankets from the students who brought them in. One credit a week was enough.

Look for Student Initiative

Well, the wheels should be spinning by now as you ponder the possibilities of paying credits to recognize and reinforce different behaviors, attitudes, and achievements.

Something to remember, though, is the initiative factor. Although offering a credit to buy a book from a student is a bit like dangling a credit from a string, I tried to avoid those kinds of situations as much as possible.

Teacher
    In an attempt to get the class to act responsibly:
        If you all walk to the auditorium quietly, I'll pay you each a credit.

Sadly, the credit that was created to be a reward has now become a bribe. And although it is somewhat similar to paying a credit to rent a blanket or buy a book, the difference is the focus. In the teacher example above, the focus was the desired behavior. In the other two, the focus was the individual student who might respond to my offer. It's subtle, but there is a psychological difference between the two.

A Student Has Earned 15 Credits

I mentioned earlier that it took a couple of weeks of paying credits before a student was

---

[†]   "Staff meeting" is one of the entries in the class glossary contained in the back of the *New Management Handbook*. *Staff meeting* was the term we used for our class meeting. Since we normally talked about administrative things—turning in forms for the office, collecting permission slips, announcing assemblies or meetings—I felt that *staff meeting* had a better ring to it than *class meeting*. As Thoreau told us back on page 32: "Language is a volatile truth." Call your five minutes of info sharing a staff meeting and it sounds a bit more significant.

able to accumulate the required 15 credits for lunch. That was partly due to how many students lost their original cards and had to start over. The main reason, though, was that I didn't make a big effort to pay credits. We had too many other, more significant, things that required our attention. Truth be told, the Credit Card program was only supposed to be a tiny part of our day. I couldn't let it become the focus of our interactions. It was something we were doing; just not the most important thing we were doing.

Nonetheless, there came that day when a student hit the magic number.

STUDENT
   Gleefully:
   Mr. Morris, I have 15 credits!

MR. MORRIS
   Fabulous. Let me see your card.
   Taking the card with a big smile:
   Nice job.
   Giving the card back along with an invitation to lunch:
   Take your card home and show your parents. I'm sure they'll want to see it. Also, have one of them sign the card so I'll know that they're aware of the lunch we're going to have in the classroom.

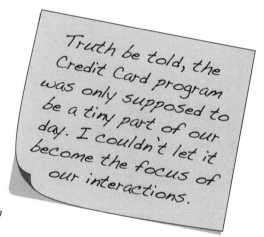

> *For the record:* There's nothing terribly important about having an adult sign the Credit Card; but, it does present an opportunity for the student to share with his parents the success he is having in the classroom. That kind of word-of-mouth advertising about the positive impact you are having on your students is well worth the effort of asking for a signature.

power
love
fun
freedom
safety

When the card was brought back to class, it was stapled to our Wall of Fame bulletin board.[†] The student was then given a new Credit Card.

MR. MORRIS
   With appreciation:
   Thanks for bringing back your card. It sure looks good up there on the Wall.
   Extending the new card:
   Here's your new card. If you can earn 15 credits before we have our lunch, you'll be able to invite a friend to join us.

power
love
fun
freedom
safety

The guest might have been a student from our room who hadn't gotten to 15 credits or a friend from another classroom. (Check with the guest's teacher.) We also had a mom, a dad, and even a grandparent. Anyone the child wanted to invite was fine with me.

---

† The Wall of Fame bulletin board is described in the *Tools & Toys* book.

A Placemat for Lunch

I bought a pack of 100, scallop-edged placemats from Smart & Final for a buck. When a student had earned 15 credits, he was given a placemat to decorate and bring to the lunch. It was a little thing, I know, but it sure added to their anticipation.

Lunch Day

By the time the day for our lunch had arrived, there were six or seven students who had earned their 15 credits. That was one of the reasons I suggested you schedule your first lunch a month after starting the Credit Card program. By waiting that long, you're almost guaranteed of having more than one student at lunch with you. (Lunch with just one can be like a bad date.) It's a more festive event when a number of students attend.

The other reason, which I didn't mention, is that the month-long wait for lunch will relieve you of the pressure of having to pay out a lot of credits quickly. Again, the whole credit thing needs to be kept in perspective. By giving yourself—and your students—a month in which to work toward the goal of 15 credits, you'll make life a lot easier in your classroom.

Early Dismissal

Since I did not provide the actual lunch—it does say BYOL (bring your own lunch) on the invitation—some of the students needed to go to the cafeteria a bit early to pick up a school lunch. I usually sent the entire lunch group even though some of them had brought in a brown bag lunch. They were going to be so giddy about the lunch anyway, that I may as well get them out of the classroom for a minute or two so I could wrap up the morning for the other students and get them to lunch on time.

Lunch Prep

There wasn't much to it. I'd bring out the ice chest in which I'd stored the drinks. I'd put on some music while they set out their placemats and organized their things. One time we lit some candles which then became part of the lunch routine. Another time a student brought in appetizers and passed them around. My last class liked to have lunch outside on the blankets, kind of like a picnic.

All-in-all, it was a pretty casual, low-key affair. They derived most of their joy from having lunch in the presence of someone they looked up to—their teacher—in a place that was not where they normally ate—their classroom.

After Lunch

As they began to finish eating, I'd set out a plate of cookies or some simple dessert. At that point, the students were free to go outside for lunch recess or stay inside and hang out with me until the bell rang for class to resume.

And that was that. A handful of students were rewarded for their behavior and achievement by their teacher who cared enough about them to expend the energy to encourage their efforts and not buy them off with a trinket but with time, the most precious gift of all.

As we look back to calculate the costs, this is what we see.

One self-inking star stamp from Staples...............$7
An ice chest stocked with juice boxes...............$5
A bag of Chips Ahoy cookies for dessert...............$4
The simple joy of eating lunch with your students...............priceless

Beyond the First Lunch

At this point, you have a couple of choices. You can either continue the Credit Card program and schedule another lunch, or you can collect everyone's card and hold off on credits for a month or two.

Continue the Credit Card Program

Since there will most likely be a majority of students in your room who did not get to attend your first lunch, you'll want to announce the new lunch date as soon as possible. What they're going to enjoy hearing from you is that the next lunch is just two weeks away. Although the first lunch occurred after a month of using Credit Cards, the second one can be moved up. If you think of all the students who are already more than halfway to 15 credits, you'll realize two weeks is optimal. It will be far enough after the first lunch to make it special but close enough to minimize any impatience.

Hold Off For a Month

There's nothing wrong with shutting down credits for a month. Although you're going to hear some whining from a few students, don't let it bother you. Some of them have been conditioned to whine at the drop of a hat.

power
love
fun
freedom
safety

During the month off, you might want to give coupons or team points a shot. Either one can be a nice change of pace. In fact, you could do coupons one week and team points the next week. This will help to keep things fresh.

At the beginning of the new month, you could resurrect their cards, distribute them, and bring out your trusty credit stamp for another fun-filled romp.

Door #3

There is one other option. That's to take the Credit Card program to a whole new level. Check the website (www.newmanagement.com) for a downloadable teaching guide entitled, *Credit Cards: Level Two.* It's a kick.

Credit Tips

As I mentioned earlier, the experience I gained using Credit Cards helped to make it better. Some of what I learned was included in this chapter. (I can honestly tell you, though, that my first experience with credits was not nearly as smooth as my last one was. But that's how it goes. We live and learn.)

Here, then, are three suggestions to help you avoid the trial-and-error I went through.

Upgrade Your Credit Stamp

Before I embellished my little credit stamp, I found myself looking for it more times than I care to recall. It would be hiding under papers, resting nearly invisible on my needing-to-be-cleaned desk, or waiting patiently for me in any number of places.

To fix the problem of not being able to find it easily, I made it more visible. My first effort was to tie a neon-colored shoelace around it. That made it possible to hang it from the post of my overhead projector. Then I added a baby toy shaped like a baseball. This made it difficult for my little stamp to hide under something. Now, all it took was a quick scan of the room to locate it. Excellent.

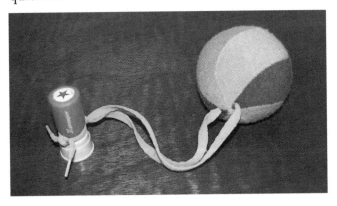

Fig. 8-7
The shoelace leash and attached baby rattle made the credit stamp so much easier to locate.

An additional advantage to having the baby toy attached to the shoelace leash, I learned, was the noise it made. The little jingling noise of the tiny bell inside the toy alerted my students to the fact that Mr. Morris was wandering around the room just looking for noteworthy behavior.

They also knew not to look up as I came near. Anyone who looked up and got off-task because of the sound of the bell didn't get paid for anything. It was actually not as harsh as it sounds. Especially not when Mr. Morris began to sound like the ice cream man coming through the neighborhood.

Alternate Credit Payments

You will soon discover that there will be times when it is not convenient to pay a credit to a student. I can think of two situations when this might be the case.

★ <u>Student can't find his Credit Card:</u> I loved to walk around the room while the students were working independently and pay students who were engaged in the task or otherwise exhibiting role model behavior. Here's the rub, though. I'd say, "Card, please." The student then proceeded to locate the card in his junk-yard-of-a-desk. I'd wait a beat and then move on. I couldn't allow myself to be held hostage to a student's lack of organization.

What often happened was that I'd be three desks away when the student suddenly announced, "I found it."

Mr. Morris
Visualizing the parents in the room:
Good. Now hang onto it so I can pay you next time.

★ <u>Students didn't have access to their Credit Cards:</u> When the students were sitting on the carpet for a lesson, they wouldn't have their Credit Cards with them. The work-around to this problem was to come up with a way to pay credits that didn't require the students' cards to be present. So, I drew upon my awareness of the power of classroom money—discussed on page 164—and made some paper credits.

Paper credits:
1. Take a sheet of colored construction paper and cut it on the paper cutter so that you end up with 3-inch squares.
2. Stamp a credit on each one of the squares.

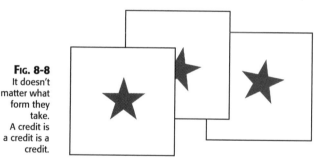

FIG. 8-8
It doesn't matter what form they take. A credit is a credit is a credit.

3. Use the paper credits in lieu of your credit stamp to pay students.
After you begin to think about it, you'll realize that this technique would also work in other settings. Whether you're on a field trip, visiting the school library, or attending an assembly, paper credits would be an ideal way to pay your students.

4. Later on, when you have the time, allow them to "cash in" a paper credit for a stamp on the Credit Card.

Keep it Positive

In order for students to truly buy-in to the Credit Card program, they have to be able to trust it. The surest way to violate that trust is to take away credits for negative behavior. Although deducting credits may seem like a viable discipline tool, the loss of trust is too costly. They need to know that once they earn a credit it won't ever be taken away.

Chapter Wrap-Up

When you first try Credit Cards with your students—and I wholeheartedly encourage you to do so—please bear in mind that there will be a brief learning period for both you and your students. That's only to be expected with something new. Nonetheless, you'll soon begin to glimpse the world of motivational potential credits offer. Although it may end up being a labor of love for you, it will be something your students will remember for a long, long time. In fact, whenever I run into former students, I almost always hear the same two questions:

You still teachin'?
Well, I'm teaching teachers now. It's a bit like teaching third graders.

Do you still do those Credit Cards?
Yeah. I'm still working that Credit Card magic.

This last chapter of the book was written to acquaint you with the endless possibilities and tremendous fun of rewarding students for their efforts with nothing more than a piece of paper, a star stamp, and a desire to see the good hiding within each child.

Book Wrap-Up

Well, that's it. Another book on the shelf. And even though I offered many ideas and strategies for interacting with your students and organizing your classroom, please don't think I'm saying that everyone needs to go the way I'm going. I'm not really out to change the world. I don't have that many answers.

All I'm trying to do is get teachers, myself included, to think about what it is we're doing and why we're doing it.

It's possible that the ideas I've shared will cause you to rethink a few of the things you do in your own classroom. If that's the case—and you and your students benefit as a result—then this book will have been worth every bit of the effort it required.